365 Fascinating Facts ABOUT THE

OLD TESTAMENT

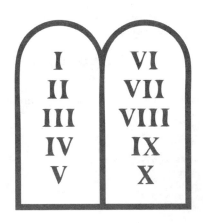

Author: Lisa Brooks

Louis Weber, CEO
Publications International, Ltd.
7373 North Cicero Avenue
Lincolnwood, Illinois 60712

Permission is never granted for commercial purposes.

ISBN-13: 978-1-4508-7583-7
ISBN-10: 1-4508-7583-1

Manufactured in U.S.A.

8 7 6 5 4 3 2 1

∞ 1 ∞

A Whale by Any Other Name ...

It's unlikely that the creature that swallowed Jonah was a whale, as is commonly believed by many. Whales are rarely sighted in the Mediterranean Sea today and were probably unknown in biblical times. Many Bible translations don't mention a whale at all, noting instead that a "great fish" or "large sea monster" swallowed Jonah.

∞ 2 ∞

Winged Messengers

The dove is best remembered as the bird that informed Noah that the waters of the Flood were receding. However, the dove wasn't the first animal released from the ark—that honor goes to the raven, which angered Noah by flying back and forth rather than doing the job it was assigned. Good PR for doves, not so much for ravens.

∞ 3 ∞

Through the River, Three Times

The Bible mentions three instances of waters being miraculously parted. The Red Sea parted when Israel, led by Moses, was fleeing the Egyptians and needed to cross. The Jordan River parted twice, first when the Israelites under Joshua needed to cross it to enter the Promised Land, and then again when the prophets Elijah and Elisha needed to cross.

☜ 4 ☞

What's in a Name?

The word *hallelujah* is Hebrew for "praise the Lord." It contains a shortened form of God's name: *Yah* (for *Yahweh*). Many biblical characters' names end similarly: Hezekiah is *chizqi-yah* ("Yahweh is my strength") and Isaiah is *yesha-yahu* ("Yahweh saves").

☜ 5 ☞

By the Letter

As bizarre as it may be, several verses in the King James Version of the Old Testament contain all letters of the alphabet but one. Ezra 7:21, for example, contains every letter except for *J*. In addition, Joshua 7:24, 1:9, 1 Chronicles 12:40, 2 Chronicles 36:10, Ezekiel 28:13, Daniel 4:37, and Haggai 1:1 contain every letter except for *Q*. And both 2 Kings 16:15 and 1 Chronicles 4:10 contain every letter except *X*.

☜ 6 ☞

Backward and Forward

Often in Hebrew, words are placed out of their natural order to produce a special impact or effect. One dramatic example is in Genesis 6:9, in the phrase "Noah walked with God." *Noah* is found at the end of the sentence; when it is read backward, the name *Enoch* is revealed. Enoch was also a famous man who "walked with God" (Genesis 5:24).

∞ 7 ∞

Permanent Records

- The longest name in the Bible is Maher-Shalal-Hash-Baz (Isaiah 8:1).

- The longest verse in the Bible is Esther 8:9. (The number of words it contains varies according to which translation you're reading, but it's a loooong sentence.)

- The longest book in the Bible is Psalms, with an impressive 150 chapters.

- The longest chapter in the Bible is Psalm 119 (a dizzying 176 verses).

∞ 8 ∞

Fear Not

The phrase "Do not be afraid" is repeated in the Bible a total of 365 times. That's one "Do not be afraid" for each day of the year (as you surely could have pieced together). Coincidence? You can decide.

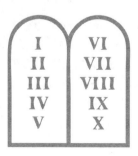

∽ 9 ∽

A Name, A Promise

When Moses asked God what his name was, God responded with this cryptic phrase: "I am who I am" (Exodus 3:14). These words in Hebrew are related to God's personal name, Yahweh. God may have been revealing something profound about himself, or he also may have been reminding Moses of his earlier promise that "I will be certainly with you" (verse 12).

∽ 10 ∽

Name Above All Names

The personal name of God (Yahweh) was so holy to the Jews that they eventually stopped pronouncing it because they felt unworthy. When they encountered this name in the scriptures while reading aloud, they substituted one of God's titles, *adonay* ("the Lord").

∽ 11 ∽

"Baboons? I Ordered Peacocks!"

Every three years, King Solomon's fleet of trading ships brought back many riches, including "baboons," according to the New International Version (2 Chronicles 9:21), or "peacocks," according to the New Revised Standard Version (2 Chronicles 9:21). The Hebrew word is either related to the Egyptian word for baboon or the Tamil word for peacock.

∞ **12** ∞
Gonna Need a Bigger Boat

All the animals did not enter Noah's ark two by two; some boarded the boat in parties of 14. These included all the birds and the clean animals that were approved for eating by Hebrew dietary law.

∞ **13** ∞
Lost Books

After describing one of Joshua's exploits, the text says, "Is this not written in the Book of Jashar?" (Joshua 10:13). Apart from two references to this book, we have no information about this historian. This also occurs with references to writings such as *The Book of the Wars of the Lord* and *The History of the Prophet Nathan*. While they were used as resources in the Old Testament, the complete works have been lost.

∞ **14** ∞
Man's Best Friend? Not Yet.

In Israel, dogs ran loose and lived as scavengers. They were despised and considered unclean by the Israelites. Proverbs 26:11 mentions a dog returning to its vomit, and, in one gruesome episode, the wicked queen Jezebel's body was eaten by dogs in the street after her death. Some dogs were kept as sheepdogs, however, and some may even have been household pets in some lands.

⌒ 15 ⌒

A Is for ... Ox?

The earliest alphabets used pictures of common objects to represent the sounds of the first letters of those words. The first letter of the Hebrew alphabet is the *aleph,* derived from *alpu* ("ox"), and so the first *aleph* was a line drawing of an ox head. Through a series of linguistic steps, it is the ancestor of the English capital *A.*

⌒ 16 ⌒

Blessings from A to Z

In Jewish tradition, God blesses Israel from "aleph to taw." These letters are the first and last in the Hebrew alphabet, so the expression means that God blesses Israel completely. By striking coincidence, the list of blessings in Leviticus 26:3–13 begins with aleph and ends with taw.

⌒ 17 ⌒

Pray Like a Lion

The Hebrew word for "meditation" (*hagah*) is also used to describe the coo of a dove, the growl of a lion, the plotting of evil rulers, and the reading of the scriptures. These things are all done audibly. Thus, when Jews were instructed to meditate on God's Word (Psalm 1:2), this meant that they should recite it aloud to themselves.

❧ **18** ❧

Say What?

The words of Adam recorded in the scriptures are in Hebrew, but he probably did not speak this language. Hebrew was not identifiable as a language until the second half of the second millennium B.C. Therefore, we do not know the precise language used by people such as Adam, Noah, or Abraham.

❧ **19** ❧

Earliest Biblical Texts

In 1979 excavators found two silver amulets. These date from about the time Jerusalem was overrun by the Babylonians in 587 B.C. What made this find special was the words inscribed on the amulets: the priestly benediction known as the Aaronic Blessing, seen in Numbers 6:22–27. That makes these artifacts the earliest biblical texts in existence today.

❧ **20** ❧

Names of God

One of God's titles was *El Shaddai*, usually translated as "God Almighty." The word *el* is a generic term for a god, used by various Semitic cultures during biblical times. So the God of Israel had to identify himself by various modifiers—God Most High (*El Elyon*), God Who Sees (*El Roi*), God Eternal (*El Olam*), and quite often *El Shaddai*, God Almighty.

❧ **21** ❧

The 611 Commandments

The Jewish rabbis counted 611 separate commandments in the law of Moses. Of those, 365 of them (one for each day of the solar year) were stated negatively, and 246 positively. In Hebrew, each letter of the alphabet corresponds to a number. Significantly, the word *Torah*, Hebrew for "law," has a numerical value of 611.

❧ **22** ❧

Symbolic Numbers

The number *one* symbolizes God's unity. "The Lord is one," declares Israel's statement of faith (Deuteronomy 6:4). *Seven* is a number of completion and perfection. God rested on the seventh day of Creation. Events often unfold in *40s*. Noah's flood took 40 days and nights, and the Israelites wandered for 40 years.

❧ **23** ❧

Camels

The camel is an ideal desert beast of burden, since it has an extraordinary ability to go long periods of time without water. The camel was domesticated about 3000 B.C., but it was not commonly used until the twelfth century B.C. We get our word *camel* from the Hebrew word *gamal*.

24

The Writing on the Wall

In Daniel 5, the Babylonian king Belshazzar saw a hand writing words on the wall. The cryptic message said, "*Mene, Mene, Tekel, Peres.*" Only Daniel was able to interpret the graffiti: *numbered, numbered, weighed, divided.* Balshazzar's days were numbered; his kingdom wasn't worth its weight; so it would be parceled out to other nations.

25

A Great Escape

The word *exodus* means "a way out." So, as you would guess, the book by that name is an escape story. Specifically, this book tells how the Israelites left Egypt. Exodus also includes the Ten Commandments, given at Mount Sinai.

26

Taking the Blame

Did you know that the word *scapegoat* comes from the Bible? Leviticus 16 describes a ritual involving two goats. One was sacrificed as a sin offering. The other was released into the desert after Israel's sins were symbolically transferred onto its head. The King James Version calls this animal the "scapegoat" (Leviticus 16:8). Eventually, the word came to refer to anyone who takes the blame for others.

↣ **27** ↢
What Is Anti-Semitic?

Nowadays, "anti-Semitic" means prejudiced against Jews. But the word actually has a much broader meaning. The term *Semite* comes from Noah's oldest son, Shem, and refers to races that were historically considered his descendants. That group would include both Jews and Arabs. So technically, anti-Semitism is opposition to all those of Middle Eastern ethnicity.

↣ **28** ↢
Biblical Onomatopoeia

Onomatopoeia refers to words that sound like what they describe, such as "buzz" or "boom." An interesting Hebrew example refers to the "galloping, galloping" sounds of Canaanite warhorses in an Israelite victory song: "daharote, daharote" (Judges 5:22).

↣ **29** ↢
The Salt Covenant

Many people add salt to their meals as seasoning. Would it surprise you to know that the sacrifices of the Israelites were also seasoned with salt? "You shall not allow the salt of the covenant of your God to be lacking from your grain offering" (Leviticus 2:13). Salt was also in the incense used in worship (Exodus 30:35). Since salt was a preservative, it symbolized eternity.

✑ **30** ✑
Leviathan

Do crocodiles appear in scripture? Maybe. Old Testament poetry references a creature named Leviathan. Isaiah calls it "that twisted serpent...the reptile that is in the sea" (27:1). Job says, "With his terrible teeth all around. His rows of scales are his pride" (41:14–15). These descriptions lead many scholars to believe that Leviathan is the crocodile of the Nile.

✑ **31** ✑
Tools of the Trade

Shepherds had two important tools in Bible times: a rod and a staff. The staff was a long pole, sometimes bent at the end, for prodding and guiding sheep. The rod was a shorter club used to defend against predators. Both appear in the well-known Shepherd's Psalm: "Your rod and Your staff, they comfort me" (Psalm 23:4).

✑ **32** ✑
Ancient Writers

Genesis 10:10 mentions the land of Shinar. This might be another name for Sumer, a nation that dominated the Tigris and Euphrates region in the third millennium B.C. The Sumerians were the world's first literate people. They invented cuneiform—triangular symbols pressed into wet clay with a reed stylus.

∽ **33** ∾

The Rose of Sharon

In the rich love poetry of the Song of Solomon, a beloved woman compares herself to the "rose of Sharon" (2:1). What was this beautiful flower? It was actually not a rose, but probably a tulip of some kind, either *Tulipa montana* or the *Tulipa sharonensis*, which grows deep red among the grasses on the Plain of Sharon.

∽ **34** ∾

Censuses, Laws, and Journeys

The book of Numbers is about preparations for Israel to enter the land of Canaan. The people are numbered, more instructions are given, and the starts and stops of their journey to the Promised Land are detailed, including the 38 years of wandering in the wilderness.

∽ **35** ∾

The Shema

Creeds have always been important in the Christian faith, to help bring communities of believers together. Judaism has something similar. It's called the *Shema*, and it comes from Deuteronomy 6:4–9. It is a classic statement of Israel's monotheism: "Hear, O Israel, the Lord our God, the Lord is one!" Its name is derived from its first word in Hebrew, *shema*, which means "hear."

↶ **36** ↷
Anything but Boring

The dazzling Jerusalem Temple built by Solomon must have been a sight to see. The materials included tons of stone blocks; boards of cedar, olive, cypress, and algum trees; metals including gold, silver, bronze, and iron; fabrics of purple, violet, and crimson; and beautiful arrays of alabaster, antimony, onyx, and all kinds of colored and precious stones.

↶ **37** ↷
Which Way Do I Pray?

In Jewish custom, it is traditional for a person to pray facing Jerusalem. The prophet Daniel followed this custom three times a day, even though the practice landed him in a den of lions. Later, when most Jews lived west of Jerusalem, a decorated plate called a *mizrach* (literally "east") was hung on the eastern wall of homes to indicate the orientation for prayer.

↶ **38** ↷
Unique Architecture

After settling in the Promised Land, the Israelites created unique architecture to distinguish themselves from their Canaanite neighbors. Excavators have identified a particularly Israelite kind of house with one long room, and three rooms side by side, each opening into the long room. People would enter the house through the middle room, used as a courtyard.

⌘ 39 ⌘

Books That Defile the Hands

For Jewish rabbis, books that were given by divine inspiration were ones that "defiled the hands" if they were touched. This idea prevented irreverent use of the scriptures. If people had to wash their hands every time they handled scriptures, they would do so carefully and reverently.

⌘ 40 ⌘

Call the Doctor

Were there doctors in the Old Testament? Absolutely. We think of medicine as modern science, but there have always been those who specialized in healing arts. For instance, Joseph enlisted doctors to embalm his father, Jacob (Genesis 50:2). And in Israel, King Asa of Judah sought medical help when he had a foot ailment (2 Chronicles 16:12).

⌘ 41 ⌘

The Job Market

In biblical times, the primary occupations were the ones that provided the basics: food and shelter. Farmers provided food, shepherds and ranchers provided meat, skins, and wool, and fishermen made profits in coastal areas. In general, women prepared and cooked the food, and made cloth out of animal hair, which they used to make clothes and tents.

∞ 42 ∞

What Is a Cubit?

God told Noah to build the ark 300 cubits long and 50 cubits wide. A cubit was a common measurement in ancient times, based on the distance from a grown man's elbow to the tip of his middle finger. The standard cubit was approximately 17.5 inches long, which would make Noah's ark about 440 feet by 73 feet—about the size of your average football field.

∞ 43 ∞

Woman and Man

You probably noticed at an early age that the word *woman* contains the word *man*. The same thing is true in Hebrew. The word for woman, *ishshah*, contains the word for man, *ish*. According to Genesis 2:23, this is no accident. "She shall be called Woman (*ishshah*)," Adam sang, "Because she was taken out of Man (*ish*)."

∞ 44 ∞

A Lot of Birthday Candles

The first 11 chapters of Genesis sweep through millennia of human experience, and include many names you won't read elsewhere. The life spans seem incredibly long, with Methuselah topping out at 969 years. But interestingly, these long life spans all came before the great flood. Afterward, very few people lived more than 120 years.

∽ **45** ∼

Ishmael: Father of the Arabs

Arabs are considered children of Abraham, too. They generally trace their ancestry back to Ishmael, Abraham's son by his wife's Egyptian slave, Hagar. Abraham sent the mother and son away from his household at Sarah's request (Genesis 16). Shortly after, God promised Hagar that Ishmael's descendants would make a great nation (Genesis 21:13).

∽ **46** ∼

Drawn Out

When the pharaoh's daughter found a baby in a basket on the Nile, she named him Moses. His Egyptian name was probably Mose or Ramose, but in Hebrew is was Mosheh, which is similar to the word mashah ("to draw out"). In Exodus 2:10, his adoptive mother explains that she drew him out of the water. Moses later drew God's people out of slavery.

∽ **47** ∼

Ramses II: Monumental Builder

Ramses II was one of Egypt's greatest pharaohs, reigning for 67 years in the thirteenth century B.C. Many scholars believe he was the pharaoh who gave Moses such a hard time regarding the Israelites' exodus from Egypt. Ramses II built many great temples, including the astounding temple complex in the sandstone cliffs at Abu Simbel on the Nile River.

☙ **48** ☙

In the Beginning

Rabbis interpreted some words in the Hebrew Bible as actually standing for entire phrases. That is, they argued that each letter of certain words represented a different word of a phrase. The first word of the Bible, *Br'shyt* ("in the beginning") was said to represent several different phrases, one of which was "in the beginning God saw that Israel would accept the Torah."

☙ **49** ☙

Offering an Olive Branch

How did the olive branch acquire its reputation as a symbol of peace? The imagery might come from the story of Noah in Genesis 8:1–12. After the rain stopped, the floodwaters were still high. Noah sent out a dove to assess the situation, and it brought back an olive leaf, indicating that some trees were above water. So the olive branch became connected with the dove in a message of peace and renewal.

☙ **50** ☙

By the Numbers

The Old Testament contains 39 books, 929 chapters, and 23,114 verses.

∞ **51** ∞

Well Dressed

Priests' clothing was colorful and expensive (Exodus 28). Ordinary priests wore long linen tunics, turbans, and beautiful belts made of blue, purple, and scarlet cloth. The high priest wore an ornate breastplate made of gold and expensive linens. This had 12 precious stones on it—one for each tribe of Israel. The hem of his robe had small bells on it, which jingled as he walked.

∞ **52** ∞

The Sixth Sick Sheik's Sixth Sheep's Sick

The Hebrew language may not have any tongue twisters quite this difficult, but the use of assonance (successive words containing the same sounds) is common. One psalmist soothingly says, *"sha'alu shelom yerushalayim"* ("Pray for the peace of Jerusalem," Psalm 122:6). And Isaiah preached that *"pachad wapachat wapach"* ("fear and the pit and the snare") will come upon the inhabitants of the earth (Isaiah 24:17).

∞ **53** ∞

Precursor to the Temple

As the Israelites wandered through the desert, they brought along a portable place of worship. God gave the Hebrews detailed instructions for building a large tent—the tabernacle—that could be moved from place to place. The tabernacle was richly decorated with expensive fabrics, and there was a special place for the ark of the covenant and other sacred items.

∞ **54** ∞

Contradictions

The Bible may be Holy Scripture, but it still contains contradictions. For example, in Genesis, it first says that man was created after the other animals (Genesis 1:25–27). Then it says man was created before the other animals (2:18–19). In Exodus, it first says that all of the (non-Hebrew) cattle and horses in Egypt died (Exodus 9:3–6), but later it is suggested that all of the pharaoh's horses did not die (14:9).

∞ **55** ∞

What About Kilts?

Daniel 3:7 mentions the bagpipe along with many other musical instruments that were played when people fell down and worshipped Nebuchadnezzar's golden statue. This bagpipe would have been made of goatskin, with two pipes protruding out.

∽ **56** ∾

Nurses in Israel

The midwife was the Israelite equivalent of a visiting nurse or public health worker. The Hebrews had professional midwives when they lived in Egypt who refused to obey the pharaoh's orders to kill Hebrew baby boys (Exodus 1). A midwife also helped Tamar when she had trouble giving birth to twins (Genesis 38).

∽ **57** ∾

Going Barefoot

Israelite priests performed many, if not all, of their duties in the tabernacle and temple barefooted. This was because of the sacredness of the ground on which they walked. God also told Moses to remove his sandals at the burning bush: "Take your sandals off your feet, for the place where you stand is holy ground" (Exodus 3:5).

∽ **58** ∾

Bible Brings Big Box Office

The Ten Commandments, starring Charlton Heston as Moses and Yul Brynner as the Pharaoh Ramses II, was the top-grossing movie of 1956 and one of the top five highest grossing movies of the 1950s. Gross to date: $80 million. Cost to produce: A little over $13 million.

Duplica...

S ome psalms appear more t...
song of praise when God de...
Saul appears as 2 Samuel 22 and...
beginning, "The fool has said in h...
appears both as Psalm 14 and 53.

60

A Poor Father

The Bible states that David did not practice good discipline with at least one of his sons. His son Adonijah rebelliously proclaimed himself king. In 1 Kings 1:6, it says David never asked Adonijah, "Why have you done thus and so?" David never held him accountable for his bad actions.

61

No Tattoos

Leviticus 19:28 prohibits self-mutilation of any sort: "You shall not make any cuttings in your flesh for the dead, nor tattoo any marks on you." This prohibition was mainly because such self-mutilation was practiced in several pagan cultures. For example, the prophets of Baal cut themselves with knives while they were trying to get Baal to send fire down from heaven (1 Kings 18:28).

∞ **62** ∞

What Is Winnowing?

Winnowing is throwing the threshed grain into the air so the wind blows away the straw (or chaff). The heavier grains fall to the ground and are saved, after which the grain is ready for storing or selling. Psalm 1 speaks of the insignificance of the wicked in God's sight as "like the chaff which the wind drives away."

∞ **63** ∞

Beloved Solomon

Jedidiah was another name given to Solomon. It means "beloved of the Lord." After David sinned by committing adultery with Bathsheba, their child died. A second child (Solomon) was born, and one name David gave him was Jedidiah, since David had been reassured that the Lord had forgiven him and still loved him, despite his sins.

∞ **64** ∞

Female Prophets

Prophetess is used five times in the Old Testament: Miriam (Exodus 15:20); Deborah (Judges 4:4); Huldah (2 Kings 22:14); Isaiah's wife, "the prophetess" (Isaiah 8:3); and Noadiah, a prophetess who opposed Nehemiah (Nehemiah 6:14). Deborah and Huldah exercised significant responsibilities.

✂ 65 ✂
Word Links

Sometimes word links between adjacent books of the Bible can be seen, which probably accounts for their being placed together. The following phrase occurs near the end of the book of Joel: "The Lord also will roar from Zion, and utter His voice from Jerusalem" (Joel 3:16). The next book, Amos, begins with exactly the same phrase (Amos 1:2).

✂ 66 ✂
What Was Palestine?

Palestine is the term popularly used today to describe the land that the twelve tribes of Israel occupied during biblical times. Its name comes from the name *Philistine*, and in the Old Testament the term designates only their territory, *Philistia*. It has been a popular title for the Holy Land for 2,000 years.

✂ 67 ✂
A Hebrew Cryptogram

A fascinating literary device found occasionally in the Hebrew Bible is called *atbash*. It created code words by substituting the first letter of the alphabet for the last, the second for the next-to-last, and so on. A famous example is in Jeremiah 51:41, where *Sheshach* is a cryptogram for Babylon.

∞ **68** ∞

A Tiny Plague

The third plague on the Egyptians was lice, according to many versions of the Bible. But it didn't take God's hand to make this so—lice were a very common problem during biblical times. In fact, archaeologists have found ancient combs from the region containing dead lice and their eggs.

∞ **69** ∞

Falcons

The falcon is a bird of prey. About ten species are known from Palestine. In Leviticus 11:14, falcons are mentioned as an abomination, not to be eaten. Job 28:7 speaks of their keen vision. One of the highest Egyptian gods was Horus, a falcon-god.

∞ **70** ∞

Instructions for Holy Living

The book of Leviticus contains instructions for the Levites—the clergy for whom the book is named—and others concerning holiness. Many laws relate to animal sacrifice, but every law is related in some way to the need for personal holiness and blamelessness in relationship with God and with others. It contains the famous passage about loving one's neighbor as oneself (Leviticus 19:18).

∽ 71 ∾

An Ancient Folk Song

Folk songs around the world arise from everyday life, and even the Bible records some. One was sung to commemorate a well: "Spring up, O well! All of you sing to it—The well the leaders sank, dug by the nation's nobles, by the lawgiver, with their staves" (Numbers 21:17–18).

∽ 72 ∾

A Real Numbers Game

Finding hidden meanings in numbers was called gematria, and it was often used to entertain and exhort, rather than to make serious claims about biblical meanings. The four consonants of God's name (Y-H-W-H) have numerical values of 10, 5, 6, and 5. The sum of their squares is 186, which is the numerical value of M-Q-W-M, which means "place." This reminded the rabbis that God is omnipresent (in every place).

∽ 73 ∾

A Dramatic End

Hebrew poetry can be very dramatic. The poetic description of the death of Sisera (the Canaanite general), whom Jael killed with a tent peg through his temple, shows an awful death struggle: "At her feet he sank, he fell, he lay still; At her feet he sank, he fell; Where he sank, there he fell dead" (Judges 5:27).

∽ 74 ∾

Anyone Have a Flyswatter?

God often used insects as weapons. For example, it is said that he sent swarms of hornets into the land of Canaan ahead of the Israelites to drive out their enemies. Whether this is a literal or symbolic reference remains open to debate.

∽ 75 ∾

God or gods?

Elohim is the Hebrew word for "God" and it also is the word for (foreign) "gods." It is a grammatically plural word (it means gods), but when it refers to God, it takes a singular verb. This plural form of the word for one God is sometimes called the "plural of majesty." It reflects the idea that God's attributes are so many and he is so great that no mere singular noun can do him justice.

∽ 76 ∾

The Lion and the Bees

Puzzling riddles were common in the biblical world. Only after the riddle was interpreted did its point become clear. A well-known riddle was Samson's: "Out of the eater came something to eat, and out of the strong came something sweet" (Judges 14:14). This referred to a lion he had killed and in whose carcass bees made honey. Because the riddle was answered, Samson killed 30 Philistines.

⊛ 77 ⊛

A Virtuous Woman

In the Hebrew Bible, the book of Ruth immediately follows Proverbs (rather than Judges, as it does in the Christian canon). This is probably because Proverbs ends with the great poem about the many virtues of a godly woman (Proverbs 31:10–31). Ruth is a perfect example of just such a woman.

⊛ 78 ⊛

Second Law

The title of the book of Deuteronomy means "second law." The book repeats and adds to many of the laws found in Exodus, Leviticus, and Numbers. The laws are framed by Moses' last addresses to the people of Israel, in which he reviews God's gracious dealings with them in the wilderness. Moses urges them to live faithful lives in their new land, Canaan.

⊛ 79 ⊛

How Many Books?

Early references to the Old Testament mentioned only 22 or 24 books, instead of the 39 that are found in Christian Bibles, even though their contents are identical. This is because books such as 1 and 2 Kings were counted as one. The books of the 12 minor prophets (Hosea through Malachi) were also counted as one, and called the Book of Twelve.

∞ **80** ∞

Moses' Speech

Moses—who was called upon more than once to talk of weighty matters—was likely a stutterer. In the Bible, he claims to be "slow of speech," which suggests some kind of speech impediment.

∞ **81** ∞

The Septuagint

The earliest Greek translation of the Hebrew Bible is called the Septuagint. Supposedly, 72 translators (representing six from each tribe of Israel) were convened in Alexandria, Egypt, about 250 B.C., but scholars today put its translation later, and taking place over a long period of time. This translation was needed because so many Jews throughout the Mediterranean world only spoke Greek.

∞ **82** ∞

A Different Order

Even though it has the same books as the Christian Old Testament, the Hebrew Bible arranges its contents differently. It has three sections, called the Law, the Prophets, and the Writings. The Prophets include the historical books such as 1 and 2 Samuel along with the traditional prophets, such as Isaiah. The Writings include Psalms and many other miscellaneous books, and it ends with 2 Chronicles.

⟡ 83 ⟡

Book of the Land

The book of Joshua focuses entirely on the land of Canaan and the Israelites' possession of it as the fulfillment of God's promise to Abraham. Moses' successor, Joshua, led Israel into the land, did battle with the Canaanites at Jericho and elsewhere, and portioned out the land to the 12 tribes of Israel.

⟡ 84 ⟡

Ancient Proofreader Needed

Scholars who believe that the Bible was originally written without any errors do accept that there were mistakes when it was copied. A famous instance where copying errors crept in is found in 1 Samuel 13:1. The Hebrew literally reads "Saul was one year old when he became king, and he reigned two years over Israel." Since we know that Saul became king as an adult and reigned for more than two years, this indicates that an ancient copyist missed at least two numbers.

⟡ 85 ⟡

Selective Genealogies

The Bible has many genealogies, listing generation after generation seemingly endlessly. Sometimes these genealogies are not all-inclusive, however. For instance, a list of Aaron's descendants in Ezra 7:1–5 omits six people who are found in the parallel list in 1 Chronicles 6:3–14.

◌ **86** ◌

What Is Wisdom?

Wisdom in the biblical sense refers to knowing how to live life well, in all its dimensions, including relationships with God and one's fellow human beings. The three "wisdom" books in the Bible are Job, Proverbs, and Ecclesiastes. The book of Proverbs begins by stating that "The fear of the Lord is the beginning of knowledge, but fools despise wisdom and instruction" (Proverbs 1:7).

◌ **87** ◌

Hyperbole

Hyperbole, or exaggeration, is a common poetic device in Hebrew. In describing his troubles, one psalmist says, "I sink in deep mire, where there is no standing; I have come into deep waters, where the floods overflow me" (Psalm 69:2). It is comical to imagine the poet literally holding scroll and pen above the water as he sinks out of sight!

◌ **88** ◌

Two-in-One Psalms

Some psalms now separated in the Bible originally were part of one composition. Psalms 9 and 10 contain an acrostic poem that begins with the first letter of the Hebrew alphabet in Psalm 9:1 and ends in Psalm 10:17 with the last letter. Psalms 42 and 43 share a common refrain, showing a common origin.

∞ **89** ∞

Time of Turmoil

The book of Judges tells a story of a repeated cycle of the nation's sin, enslavement, and deliverance by warrior-judges. The cycle spirals downward, however, and by the end of the book things are so bad that the author despairingly says, "in those days Israel had no king; everyone did as he saw fit."

∞ **90** ∞

Aramaic Targums

Aramaic was a sister language to Hebrew, and was used starting in the late Old Testament period. The earliest Aramaic translations of the Hebrew Bible were the Targums. They were oral paraphrases on each book, not exact translations, and they were laden with commentary and explanatory glosses. The earliest of these were committed to writing during the period between the composition of the last book of the Old Testament and the first book of the New Testament.

∞ **91** ∞

Searching for Wisdom

Job 28 contains a majestic poem about wisdom. It states that wisdom is not to be found in the deepest sea, nor can it be bought for gold, nor can any animal or human being know it on its own. Only "God understands its way, and He knows its place" (verse 23). God reveals wisdom to humans.

∞ **92** ∞

King David's Story

The books of 1 and 2 Samuel tell of the introduction of kingship in Israel under the prophet Samuel. Israel's first king, Saul, was disqualified, and David became king. Three-quarters of these books are devoted to David's rise to power and to his reign. God promised David an unbroken line of successors on the throne of the kingdom.

∞ **93** ∞

A Love Story

The book of Ruth is a literary masterpiece, a sparkling gem that tells a heartwarming story about a widowed woman (Naomi) and her daughter-in-law (Ruth), for whom things finally work out in the end. Ruth marries Boaz, who provides for them both. The family tree at the book's end connects Ruth with Abraham and shows her to be David's great-grandmother.

∞ **94** ∞

A Reverence for Scripture

In early Jewish custom, translation of the Hebrew Scriptures in the worship services could only be done orally, not read from a scroll. This probably was to preserve the distinctiveness and sacredness of the written Hebrew scriptures. It is said that the Rabbi Gamaliel, the Apostle Paul's teacher, rejected a written copy of Job and had it buried in a wall.

⟡ 95 ⟡

Head for the Center

A well-written essay usually states its objective at the beginning. Some biblical psalms, however, make their main point halfway through. These psalms are so precisely constructed that you can count the number of Hebrew words in the psalm, divide by two, and find the psalm's most important thought precisely at the midpoint. Examples include Psalms 8, 23, 95, and 100.

⟡ 96 ⟡

Israel's Songs and Prayers

The 150 psalms in the Psalter formed a hymnbook of sorts for Israel. These hymns cover the range of human emotion, from ecstatic joy to deepest despair. They have taught Jews and Christians how to sing and pray, and also convey truths about God and everyday faith and life.

⟡ 97 ⟡

The Wrong Songs

Drinking songs are part of almost every culture, and prophets Amos and Isaiah disapprovingly referred to them in biblical society. Isaiah even quotes two such songs: "Let us eat and drink, for tomorrow we die" (Isaiah 22:13). "'Come,' one says, 'I will bring wine, and we will fill ourselves with intoxicating drink'" (Isaiah 56:12).

∽ 98 ∽
Playing With Words

Hebrew writers often used similar sounding words to illustrate their ideas. The prophet Isaiah made an effective point about conditions in the land with word play: "And he [God] looked for justice (*mishpat*), but saw bloodshed (*mishpach*); for righteousness (*tsedaqah*), but heard cries of distress (*tse'aqah*)." (Isaiah 5:7, NIV)

∽ 99 ∽
The Kings of Israel and Judah

Under David's son Solomon, the nation began to crumble and eventually it split into two: northern Israel (ten tribes) and southern Judah (two tribes). The books of 1 and 2 Kings chronicle the fortunes of the two kingdoms. Israel had an unbroken succession of bad kings. Judah had the descendants of David and a mixture of good and bad kings. The books end with Israel annihilated and Judah under Babylonian captivity.

∽ 100 ∽
A Basketball Star?

The fight between David and Goliath (1 Samuel 17) is one of the Old Testament's most well-known tales. But exactly how tall was Goliath? According to the Bible, the giant stood "six cubits and a span," which is more than nine feet. (Nine-feet-two-inches plus in sandals!)

❧ 101 ❧
Cut-and-Paste Psalms

Some psalms were composed in much the same way that modern church prayer books are, by stringing together different portions of scripture to form new compositions. Psalm 108 is made up entirely of parts of Psalm 57 and 60, and the lengthy hymn of thanksgiving when the ark reached Jerusalem found in 1 Chronicles 16 is composed of poetry found in three psalms: 96, 105, and 106.

❧ 102 ❧
A Pun-ishing Experience

Speakers of Hebrew loved a good pun. The prophet Amos was once shown a vision of a basket of "(ripe) summer fruit" (Hebrew *qayits*), to illustrate the point that the "end" (Hebrew *qets*) had come for Israel—the time was "ripe" for destruction (Amos 8:2).

❧ 103 ❧
David's Kingdom

Fully half of the books of 1 and 2 Chronicles are copied word-for-word from 1 and 2 Samuel and 1 and 2 Kings, but the author presents a very different slant. He is only interested in the fortunes of David and the kingdom of Judah (which represented David's descendants), and he consistently evaluates the nation's fortunes in terms of its trust in God.

◌ **104** ◌

More Than a Fish

The message of the book of Jonah is often obscured by discussions about the fish that swallowed the prophet. It is a wonderful book about God's concern for all people, not just his chosen people. Jonah was sent to Nineveh, the capital of the world's largest empire, to urge its people to repent, and they did.

◌ **105** ◌

Baal: A God or a Husband?

The Canaanite god Baal is well known in the Bible and in other literature. His name is a generic Semitic word (*baal*) meaning "lord," "master," or "owner." A specialized use of *baal* is "husband," reflecting the idea of husbands as lords over their wives.

◌ **106** ◌

Faces and Wheels

Ezekiel had a glittering vision about four shining manlike creatures that were accompanied by four wheels (Ezekiel 1). The creatures each had four wings and four faces: a man, a lion, an ox, and an eagle. The wheels did not turn, but they had eyes in them, and they flew wherever the creatures flew. The vision portrayed God's majesty in vivid terms.

☞ **107** ☜

A Typical Prophet

Micah fits well the stereotype of a biblical prophet, speaking out against both social and spiritual evils, and also looking into the future and speaking of the restoration of God's people. He predicted that the Messiah would come from Bethlehem, and he summarized well the duties of God's people: "And what does the Lord require of you but to do justly, to love mercy, and to walk humbly with your God" (Micah 6:8).

☞ **108** ☜

Chronology and Order

In the Old Testament, the first 17 books (Genesis through Esther) are in essentially chronological order, beginning with creation and ending with the Jews in exile at the end of the Old Testament period. Other books are not grouped chronologically. The prophetic books are arranged with the three longest books first. Most of the prophets fit chronologically into the time period covered by the books of 1 and 2 Kings.

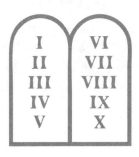

∞ 109 ∞

Long Before the Alamo

Small armies fighting against overwhelming numbers are commonplace in the Bible, but Gideon wins the prize for most unlikely victory. He fought off 135,000 Midianite invaders with just 300 soldiers and 300 trumpets.

∞ 110 ∞

A Psalm Is Still a Psalm

Besides the 150 psalms in the biblical Psalter, the Bible has many other psalms scattered throughout other books. Famous examples include psalms in Exodus 15 (Moses and Miriam's Song of the Sea), Deuteronomy 32 (Moses' song), Judges 5 (Deborah and Barak's victory song), 1 Samuel 2 (Hannah's song of praise), 2 Samuel 1 (David's lament), Jonah 2 (Jonah's prayer of thanksgiving), and Habakkuk 3 (Habakkuk's song of praise).

∞ 111 ∞

The Lady and the Harlot

The author of Proverbs uses a vivid contrast to make a point about right living. He warns his son in chapter 7 of the dangers of the seductive call of the harlot who looks out of her window. Instead the young man is urged to let himself be seduced by "Lady Wisdom" (chapter 8): "Does not wisdom cry out, and understanding lift up her voice?"

∞ 112 ∞

Guardians of the Scriptures

Hebrew was originally written without vowels, spaces between words, or punctuation. The Masoretes were Jewish scribes who first appeared in the second century A.D. They devised a system of word, phrase, sentence, and paragraph divisions, as well as a detailed system for representing the vowels and accents on words. This ensured that the Hebrew Scriptures would be uniformly copied, pronounced, and interpreted.

∞ 113 ∞

Books of Restoration

The books of Ezra and Nehemiah show the restoration of Judah after the destruction of Jerusalem and its exile in Babylon. The temple was rebuilt and Ezra and Nehemiah returned from exile to Judah to start religious and political reforms, which included rebuilding the walls of the city.

∞ 114 ∞

A Prophet Par Excellence

The book of Isaiah is arguably the greatest of the prophetic books. Its scope is all encompassing. The book ranges from dramatic criticisms of wicked Judah to tender assurances of God's love and restoration to visions of the new heavens and the new earth. Many passages from Handel's *Messiah* are taken from Isaiah.

❧ 115 ❧

When in Rome

The priest Jerome, who lived during the time of the Roman empire, was not the first to translate the Bible into Latin, but his translation became the standard. Much of his version was translated directly from the Hebrew text, rather than from previous Greek or Latin versions. Jerome's version, called the Vulgate, was used for centuries. When later translators put the Bible into different languages, they often used the Vulgate as their source.

❧ 116 ❧

Ladder to Heaven

Jacob dreamed about a ladder he saw ascending into heaven. The numerical value of the Hebrew word for ladder equals that of the word Sinai. Thus, rabbis argued that the Torah—the law of Moses—which was revealed at Mount Sinai, was the ladder that leads from earth to heaven.

❧ 117 ❧

What Is the Tanakh?

This is what Jews call their Bible, and it is the acronym for the Hebrew Bible. The word is based upon the three divisions of the Hebrew Bible: the Law, the Prophets, and the Writings. The Hebrew words for these are *Torah*, *Nebi'im*, and *Kethubim*. The first letters of these three words, T-N-K, come together in the word Tanakh.

❦ 118 ❦

A Glaring Omission

Two books in the Bible do not mention God even once: the love poetry of the Song of Solomon, and the book of Esther, which tells of the Jewish people's life and successes under Persian rule.

❦ 119 ❦

Psalm Titles

The majority of the psalms (116 in all) have titles that were added in antiquity. Many attribute the psalm to a certain author (David, Asaph, sons of Korah), while many classify the psalm (as a prayer, a praise, a *maskil*, a *miktam*, a *shiggaion*). Some contain musical instructions ("For the choir director"), while others have historical notes ("A Psalm of David, when Nathan the prophet came to him after he went into Bathsheba").

❦ 120 ❦

A Living Language

The Old Testament was written over a period of 1,000 years, primarily in Hebrew. The language changed over that time and occasionally needed to be updated. One example of this is in 1 Samuel 9:9: "Formerly in Israel, when a man went to inquire of God, he spoke thus: 'Come, let us go to the seer,' for he who is now called a prophet was formerly called a seer."

∽ **121** ∾

A Loquacious Prophet

Although Psalms has the most chapters of any book in the Bible (150), the book of Jeremiah (with a mere 52 chapters) has the most words. Jeremiah was a passionate prophet, pouring out his heart at great length and with great emotion to God.

∽ **122** ∾

Reminders of Responsibility

The book of Ezekiel contains many strange visions and strange actions. His message was to the Jews in Babylonian exile, helping them to make sense of their punishment and pointing them to a way of restoration. Along with Jeremiah, he emphasized the concept of each individual's responsibility for his or her own sin, a concept that had been forgotten in Judah. His book ends with a great vision of the ideal temple.

∽ **123** ∾

A Philosophic Book

The book of Ecclesiastes is written by someone who has tried everything in search for meaning in life, but come up empty. It is full of frustration, even cynicism, but the book ends by affirming that life has meaning when lived in right relation with God. It is the closest piece of writing in the Bible to what the Greeks called philosophy.

∽ 124 ∽
Why Do We Suffer?

The book of Job is one of the world's classics on the question of human suffering. Job, an innocent man who feared God, is put through much suffering. Through this, Job passionately questions God but he never abandons belief in God. After a direct encounter with God, Job's questions cease and his fortunes are fully restored.

∽ 125 ∽
Books Within a Book

The book of Psalms is organized into five books, consisting of Psalms 1–41, 42–72, 73–89, 90–106, and 107–150. Each of these concludes with a short doxology, praising God, and the word amen. The Jewish Midrash (commentary) on the Psalms, written in the tenth century A.D., equates this division with that of the Pentateuch: "As Moses gave five books of law to Israel, so David gave five books of Psalms to Israel."

∽ 126 ∽
Poetic Laments

Perhaps the most emotional book in the Bible is the book of Lamentations, which has five chapters of anguished laments over the destruction of Jerusalem. Strangely, these heartfelt laments are expressed in the rigid structure of the acrostic: each chapter has 22 verses (or a multiple of 22).

∽ 127 ∾

The Day of the Lord

The short book of Joel focuses on the concept of the "Day of the Lord." This sometimes refers to God's immediate judgment on nations that oppressed others (such as in a great locust plague), and sometimes refers to God's judgment of all nations at the end of time.

∽ 128 ∾

Love Songs

The Song of Solomon, also called the Song of Songs, is a beautiful collection of love poetry, much of which is rather explicit, even erotic. Some Jews and Christians have seen in the book a description of God's relationship with Israel or the Christian Church, and thereby avoided some of their embarrassment about the language of love.

∽ 129 ∾

Books of Passion

The prophet Jeremiah revealed his personal passions more than any other prophet. He wept bitterly over the sins of his people and argued bitterly with God for sending him as a prophet. He was vigorously opposed by false prophets and suffered much for his stand. Lamentations also includes passionate laments over the destruction of Jerusalem, traditionally ascribed to Jeremiah.

∽ 130 ∾

The Most Expensive Bible

The world's most expensive Bible is the copy of Gutenberg's Old Testament, containing Genesis through Psalms. It was printed in 1455, and it brought $5.39 million at an auction at Christie's in New York on October 22, 1987.

∽ 131 ∾

Creation

An Israelite obviously didn't write the famous poem that contains the words, "Only God can make a tree." The Hebrew language has a special word, *bara*, which refers to God's creative acts. In Hebrew, humans can form, make, and build, and so can God, but only God can create. Since the materials out of which God creates are never mentioned with the word *bara*, we know that God creates out of nothing.

∽ 132 ∾

Be Strong

God encouraged Joshua by telling him to be strong and courageous (Joshua 1:6–7, 9). In Jewish tradition, after any of the five books of Moses is read publicly in the synagogue, the congregation rises and proclaims, "Be strong! Be strong! And let us take courage!" This refers to the courage to live according to the teachings in these books.

❧ 133 ❧

A Rabbi's Good Advice

Constant study of the Law was very important in the Jewish community. Psalm 1:2 states that the righteous person's delight is in meditating day and night on the Law. The great rabbi Hillel encouraged frequent repetition in such study by saying that "reviewing a lesson a hundred times cannot be compared with reviewing it a hundred and one times."

❧ 134 ❧

Twenty-Four Fingers and Toes?

A Philistine giant mentioned in 1 Chronicles 20:6 had six fingers on each hand and six toes on each foot. This phenomenon (called polydactylism) is commonly known from ancient texts and art. In an early temple in Jericho, a six-toed clay statue was found. In Assyria, a child with six fingers on the left hand was considered a good sign, but six fingers on the right hand was a sign of bad fortune.

❧ 135 ❧

A Real Number Cruncher

The book of Proverbs contains many proverbs of Solomon, including one section entitled "The Proverbs of Solomon" (Proverbs 10:1—22:16). In this section there are exactly 375 proverbs. Not coincidentally, the numerical value of Solomon's name is 375.

⟐ 136 ⟐

Hidden Books

The word *apocrypha* means "hidden," and it usually refers to 12 or more books added to the 39 books of the Hebrew Bible. These were written between 200 B.C. and A.D. 100, and are considered by many Christians to be part of the Bible since most were found in the first Greek translations of the Hebrew Bible. The Roman Catholic Church accepts 12 additional books, while Eastern Orthodox churches accept 4 to 5 books beyond that.

⟐ 137 ⟐

God Hidden in Esther

Even though God is not mentioned directly in the book of Esther, the Jewish rabbis did find his name in the book, hidden in an acrostic. The first letters of four succeeding Hebrew words at a crucial point in the book are the same four letters that form the basis for God's holy name: Y-H-W-H (Yahweh). The rabbis felt that God still maintained an unseen presence in the book.

∞ 138 ∞

A Roll of the Dice

The festival of Purim got its name from a rare word meaning "lot" (Hebrew *pur*). This festival celebrates the reversal of events that had been determined by Haman, the Jews' enemy, by casting lots or dice. An example of such a die, from Assyria, was found recently, dating to the ninth century B.C. It is a small, six-sided clay cube with the word *pur* on it.

∞ 139 ∞

Dentists in the Bible?

The prophet Amos, like most of the prophets, often used picturesque language to make his point. In one passage, to illustrate that God had used famine to try to jolt Israel out of its spiritual lethargy, he says that God gave Israel "cleanness of teeth" (Amos 4:6). This is not a reference to personal hygiene, but instead means they had no food to get between their teeth.

∞ 140 ∞

Behemoths

The Hebrew word *behemoth* is a rare word for "beasts." In Job 40:15, it refers to a large animal, probably the hippopotamus. Many English versions merely render it as behemoth, however. The modern-day meaning of something large (football players as behemoths) takes its meaning from this passage.

∽ **141** ∾

The Shortest Chapter in the Bible

The Bible's shortest chapter, Psalms 117, comes just two chapters before its longest chapter. It is a beautiful little gem, a burst of praise to God, urging people to praise God for his goodness and faithfulness. It is only two verses long!

∽ **142** ∾

Psalms for a Pilgrimage

Fifteen consecutive psalms have the title "A Psalm of Ascents": Psalms 120 to 134. Rabbinic tradition states that there were fifteen steps going up from the Women's Court in the temple to the Israelites' Court, and that a psalm was composed for each. More likely, these psalms were composed for the pilgrimage up to Jerusalem, "the mountain of the Lord" (Isaiah 30:29).

∽ **143** ∾

A Visionary Prophet

The book of Daniel contains an equal mixture of stories about Daniel and his friends in exile—such as Daniel in the lion's den or his three friends (Shadrach, Meshach, and Abednego) in the fiery furnace—and of visions about the future. The common thread between both parts of the book is the idea of God's control of the world's empires and his vindication of his people.

∽ **144** ∾

A Second Language

While most of the Old Testament was written in Hebrew, several chapters in Ezra and Daniel (and even one verse in Jeremiah) were written in Aramaic. These sections come in contexts where international affairs are concerned, and the writers felt it helpful to write in the lingua franca of the day.

∽ **145** ∾

The Apple of Your Eye

This phrase is found five times in the King James Version of the Bible, including the prayer "Keep me as the apple of your eye." In reality, the Hebrew word here means "pupil (of the eye)," and the idea is one of God's keeping close watch over his people. Hebrew has a separate word for the fruit.

∽ **146** ∾

Joseph and the Amazing Technicolor Dream Coat

While this makes a good title for a Broadway musical, and the story of Jacob giving his favorite son a multicolored coat paints a gripping picture, the reference to the coat's color is not necessarily accurate. Most recent Bible versions render the phrase as a "richly ornamented robe," "an ornamented tunic," or "a long robe with sleeves."

∽ **147** ∾

A Thorn in Israel's Side

When Israel inherited the land of Canaan, one of its top priorities was to drive out the Canaanites, who worshipped many pagan gods. God repeatedly warned them of the dangers of mixing with them. At one point, he stated that they would be "irritants in your eyes and thorns in your sides" (Numbers 33:55).

∽ **148** ∾

The Tale of the Tel

The Hebrew word *tel* refers to a layered mound that has been built up over the centuries by successive occupations. Most large cities in Palestine were rebuilt on the same locations, and the remains of their mounds can still be seen today. The translators of the King James Bible had never seen a tel, and thus they mistranslated Joshua 11:13, which refers to "cities that stood on their mounds (tels)" as "cities that stood still in their strength."

∽ **149** ∾

Obadiah: Edom's Doom

This shortest book in the Old Testament is a brief but concentrated blast of condemnation at Judah's neighbor Edom, located southeast of the Dead Sea. Edom had rejoiced at Jerusalem's downfall, and this book speaks about that.

∽ 150 ∽
An Eye for the Numbers

The Masoretes, the Jewish scribes who painstakingly copied the Hebrew scriptures, were so precise in their copying that they counted the number of words in each book of their Bibles, and even identified the middle word. They did this so they could check themselves and be sure they had not accidentally skipped any words.

∽ 151 ∽
The Wicked Bible

Some humorous typographical errors were made in early editions of the King James Bible. Probably the most famous was the omission of the word "not" in the seventh commandment, and thus it read, "Thou shalt commit adultery." This edition was dubbed the Wicked Bible. For this error, the King's printers were fined 300 pounds by the archbishop!

∽ 152 ∽
A Social Conscience for Israel

More than any prophet, Amos spoke out against social evils, such as abuse of power, oppression of the poor, dishonest dealings, and insincere religious ritual. He even spoke out against the life of leisure, and the many possessions and the summer homes of the wealthy. These luxuries blinded the people to the very real needs around them.

∽ 153 ∾

An Egyptian Reference to Israel

The earliest reference to Israel outside of the Bible dates to about 1208 B.C., at a time when Israel had settled into the land of Canaan after following Moses out of Egypt. The Egyptian pharaoh Merneptah boasted in a victory song that he had defeated many of his enemies, including Israel: "Israel is laid waste, his seed is not."

∽ 154 ∾

Practical Wisdom

The book of Proverbs is one of the most practical books in the Bible, with its common-sense approach to life. This is captured in hundreds of short, pithy sayings (proverbs) about how to live well in all dimensions, with God and our neighbors.

∽ 155 ∾

A Jewish Traitor?

Jeremiah emphasized strongly that the Jews should not resist the Babylonians, since they were God's instrument to punish Judah's sins. Many in Jerusalem, however, did not like this counsel. They accused Jeremiah of being a traitor, saying, "he weakens the hands of the men of war who remain in this city… This man does not seek the welfare of this people, but their harm" (Jeremiah 38:4).

∽ 156 ∽

Biblical Acrostics

Highly structured Hebrew poetry found its most specialized expression in the acrostic poem, where each succeeding verse in the poem began with succeeding letters of the Hebrew alphabet, 22 in all. Psalms 25, 34, 37, 111, 112, 119, and 145 are all examples of this. The poem extolling the virtues of a godly woman in Proverbs 31:10–31 is also an acrostic.

∽ 157 ∽

Can You Keep a Secret?

The book of Daniel contains explicit words about the book's focus: Much of it was not for the present, but for a future time. Daniel was instructed in a vision to "seal up the vision, for it refers to many days in the future" (Daniel 8:26) and to "seal the book until the time of the end" (Daniel 12:4).

∽ 158 ∽

Another Flood Story

Many versions of flood stories exist in the ancient Near East. The most famous tells of a legendary king, Gilgamesh, on a quest for eternal life. Along the way he meets Ut-napishtim, who has been given the gift of immortality by the gods. Ut-napishtim was a hero of old who had survived a flood, like Noah, by building a boat. Many details are similar to the biblical flood story.

✇ 159 ✇

The Oldest Hebrew Bible

The oldest complete version of the Hebrew Bible still in existence dates from A.D. 1008. It is part of a comprehensive collection of old Hebrew manuscripts in the Russian Public Library in St. Petersburg (formerly Leningrad), brought there in the late 1800s. It is known as the Leningrad Codex.

✇ 160 ✇

No More Homework, No More Books

The author of Ecclesiastes voiced the complaints of endless generations of students when he said, "Of making many books there is no end, and much study is wearisome to the flesh" (Ecclesiastes 12:12). His point was that fearing God and pleasing him are what bring true fulfillment.

✇ 161 ✇

Carved in Stone

The most important documents in antiquity were laboriously carved into stone, so they were permanent. The Ten Commandments were written on two stone tablets. The Babylonian king Hammurabi's Law Code was written on a hard diorite stone stele. The Moabite king Mesha's inscription regarding his war with Israel was inscribed on a large black basalt stone.

⌒ **162** ⌒

Same Verse, Different Number

In many places, the verse numbering in the English Old Testament differs slightly from that in the Hebrew Bible, even though the contents are exactly the same. Most often this happens in Psalms, where English Bibles do not number the titles of the ancient psalms, while the Hebrew Bible does.

⌒ **163** ⌒

The Fall of Jerusalem

The most traumatic event for Israel in the Old Testament was the destruction of Jerusalem in 586 B.C. by the Babylonians under Nebuchadnezzar (2 Kings 25). The city was razed, the temple looted and destroyed, most of the people carried into exile, and a puppet ruler set up over the land. Even the great bronze pillars in front of the temple were carried away.

⌒ **164** ⌒

Who Gets Credit?

The Bible tells of the Assyrian king Shalmaneser's conquest of Samaria in 722 B.C., in 2 Kings 17. However, in the Assyrian annals, King Sargon II, Shalmaneser's successor, claims the credit. The problem may be resolved by assuming that Shalmaneser was still king, but his general Sargon actually took the city.

∽ 165 ∾

The End of a Language

Hebrew began to die out as a spoken language toward the end of the Old Testament period, partly as a result of the Jews' intermarriage and assimilation. Nehemiah was distressed to find Jews who had married foreign women and whose children could not speak "the language of Judah" (Hebrew).

∽ 166 ∾

Philistine Behavior

The word "philistine" has come to mean uncultured or boorish in English. This is because of the mostly negative presentation in the Bible of the Philistines, who were Israel's major enemy between 1150 and 1000 B.C. The Philistine culture, however, was fairly advanced in political organization and especially in the arts.

∽ 167 ∾

The Writing of God

The Bible claims to be the Word of God. However, some passages mention God's writing explicitly. The Ten Commandments were "written with the finger of God" (Exodus 31:18); they were "the writing of God" (Exodus 32:16). In 1 Chronicles 28:19, David said, "The Lord made me understand in writing, by his hand upon me, all the works of these plans."

∞ 168 ∞

A Strange Famine

The prophet Amos gives a startlingly vivid picture of what conditions would soon be like in Israel because of its rejection of the Lord: "I will send a famine on the land; not a famine of bread, nor a thirst for water, but of hearing the words of the Lord. They shall wander from sea to sea, and from north to east; they shall run to and fro, seeking the word of the Lord, but they shall not find it" (Amos 8:11–12).

∞ 169 ∞

What Is Sheol?

The Hebrew term *sheol* occurs 65 times in the Old Testament, referring to the place of the dead. The King James Version translates it "hell" 31 times, the "grave" 31 times, and the "pit" 3 times. While meaning merely the grave at times, sometimes it seems to refer more to a shadowy realm of the dead. The full-blown concept of hell as a place of punishment is not developed in the Old Testament.

∞ 170 ∞

Book Burning

Book burning isn't just a modern-day occurrence. The Bible mentions that King Jehoiakim of Judah burned the book of Jeremiah in the fire that was on the hearth, "until all the scroll was consumed in the fire" (Jeremiah 36:23).

∽ 171 ∽

All Sins Are Forgiven

Psalm 32 is a beautiful reflection on the joys of having one's sins forgiven. It uses no fewer than four words for sin in its opening lines: "Happy are those whose *transgression* is forgiven, whose *sin* is covered. Happy are those to whom the Lord imputes no *iniquity*, and in whose spirit there is no *deceit*." The variety of terms used creates the solid assurance that whatever the sin, it is covered and forgiven.

∽ 172 ∽

In Good Company

Many people know that Methuselah was the oldest man in the Bible, living 969 years. However, he was not unique for his time. Jared lived for 962, Noah lived for 950 years, Seth lived for 912 years, Enosh lived for 905 years, and Mahalalel lived for 895 years. The first man, Adam, lived for 930 years.

∽ 173 ∽

Shooting Arrows

The Hebrew verb that is related to the noun Torah is *yarah*, which means, "to shoot an arrow." The relationship between the two is that the Torah points in the right direction, aimed toward the mark of a right relationship with God. Interestingly enough, one of the major words for sin in Hebrew (*chata*) means, "to miss the mark."

174

Censorship

The first chapter of the book of Ezekiel may have portrayed God's majesty, but it was very strange. In fact, it was so difficult and so strange that Jewish young people under the age of 30 were not allowed to read it!

175

An Eye for an Eye

The penalties stated in Exodus 21:23–25 concerning an eye for an eye or a life for a life sound barbaric to many people today. However, the principle was very humane: Let the punishment fit the crime. In the ancient Near Eastern world, this limited the usual cycle of escalating retribution and revenge.

176

What Is a Helpmate?

This usually refers to a wife, in her role as helper to her husband. The word has arisen from the King James Version's rendering of two Hebrew words in Genesis 2:18, where God says, "I will make [Adam] an help meet for him." However, "meet" in seventeenth-century English meant, "appropriate" or "fit for." So helpmate was not originally a true word; modern versions usually translate the phrase "a helper fit for him."

❧ **177** ❧

Did He Remember Their Names?

King Solomon must have been exhausted. According to the Bible, Solomon had 700 wives and more than 300 concubines. The biggest question: How did he remember all his wedding anniversaries?

❧ **178** ❧

The Calves of Our Lips

In Hosea 14:2, the King James Version states that God's people would respond to his grace by offering "the calves of our lips." Most modern versions have "the fruit of our lips" (meaning praises to God). The Hebrew is paraphrased as "we shall offer the praise of our lips in place of sacrificial bullocks." This means that praise, not sacrifice, is the valued offering.

❧ **179** ❧

The Language of Diplomats

Just as English is the international language of trade and diplomacy (or the *lingua franca*) in most of the world today, so Aramaic was during the time of Israel's monarchy. The Assyrian king Sennacherib's emissaries insulted King Hezekiah's envoys during the siege of Jerusalem by issuing demands in the local language, Hebrew, in full hearing of the common people. This was despite the envoy's request that the negotiations be conducted in Aramaic, for secrecy's sake (2 Kings 18:26–35).

∞ **180** ∞

Chariots of the Sun

King Josiah removed the "horses that the kings of Judah had dedicated to the sun" from the entrance to the temple, and he burned their "chariots of the sun" with fire as part of his great reform movement (2 Kings 23:11). Worship of the sun god was common in the ancient Near East, and several cultures depicted him as a charioteer riding across the sky pulling the sun behind him.

∞ **181** ∞

Love Is Confusing

Among the proverbs of Agur in Proverbs 30 is a list of four things he does not understand: "the way of an eagle in the air, the way of a serpent on a rock, the way of a ship in the midst of the sea, and the way of a man with a virgin" (verse 19).

∞ **182** ∞

Beautiful Feet

The prophet Isaiah painted an exquisite word picture of comfort for Jerusalem when he stated: "How beautiful on the mountains are the feet of those who bring good news, who proclaim peace, who bring good tidings, who proclaim salvation, who say to Zion, 'Your God reigns!'" (Isaiah 52:7, NIV). The focus on the feet of messengers adds to the impact of the uplifting message.

❧ **183** ❧

Ancient Law Codes

The Mosaic law contains 613 specific commandments regulating most aspects of people's lives and worship, but this is not the earliest example of an ancient law code. The Sumerians developed the first such codes in the middle of the second millennium B.C. The most systematic law code was that of the Babylonian king Hammurabi (1792–1750 B.C.). The Hittites also developed an extensive law code in the thirteenth century B.C.

❧ **184** ❧

What Does Selah Mean?

Selah is a Hebrew term found 71 times in the book of Psalms and three times in a psalm in Habakkuk. It usually comes at the end of a poetic stanza. Scholars do not know its exact meaning, but it is probably a musical or liturgical instruction of some type, such as pause or crescendo.

❧ **185** ❧

A Grim Parallel

In Genesis 40, Joseph tells Pharaoh's butler in prison that Pharaoh will "lift up your head and restore you to your place." He tells Pharaoh's baker that Pharaoh will "lift off your head from you and hang you on a tree." His predictions of rescue for one man and death for the other were accurate.

∞ **186** ∞

Am I My Brother's Keeper?

This is the response of Cain—who killed his brother Abel—when God came to him and asked him where Abel was (Genesis 4:9). He was attempting to deflect or escape responsibility for his crime. People wanting to avoid responsibility often use the phrase today.

∞ **187** ∞

Raising Ebenezer

A well-known hymn written in the eighteenth century and still in use today contains the line, "Here I raise mine Ebenezer." Ebenezer is a Hebrew term meaning "stone of help." After a victory over the Philistines, Samuel set up a memorial stone and called it Ebenezer because the Lord had helped Israel.

∞ **188** ∞

Nothing New Under the Sun

The author of Ecclesiastes uses the phrase "under the sun" more than 25 times, as he expresses weariness with life. In his search for fulfillment, he discovers that: "What has been will be again, what has been done will be done again; there is nothing new under the sun" (Ecclesiastes 1:9, NIV). He concludes that the search for something new is misguided, that fulfillment comes in fearing God.

∽ 189 ∾

The Nuzi Tablets

More than 4,000 clay tablets were discovered in the 1920s at ancient Nuzi, east of the Tigris River. These date to the middle of the second millennium B.C. These texts give a wide-ranging picture of everyday life at that time, including things such as land ownership, the position of slaves and women, prices and sales of goods, occupations, legal customs, and family law. Many intriguing parallels are found in Genesis and the Nuzi documents.

∽ 190 ∾

Heavenly Library

In many passages, the Bible refers to books kept in heaven. Moses pleads with God to blot him out of the "book which you have written" (Exodus 32:32) for the sake of Israel's forgiveness. The book of Daniel speaks of the day when "the books were opened" (Daniel 7:10). And the book of Malachi speaks of a "book of remembrance" that was written about those who feared the Lord (Malachi 3:16).

❧ 191 ❧

Animals and Humans

Genesis 1 and 2 tell us that God created animals before humans, that he gave humans responsibility to be good stewards over the animals, and that Adam gave names to them. Originally, humans were vegetarians, but after Noah's Flood, God gave animals for food as well. Animals also were used for transportation, in working the fields, as sacrificial animals, in the military, and as pets.

❧ 192 ❧

From Dust to Dust

The words "Ashes to ashes, dust to dust" are often spoken at the gravesite during a funeral. The term is adapted from God's words to Adam in Genesis 3:19, reminding him that he was formed out of the ground and would return there: "for dust you are, and to dust you shall return."

❧ 193 ❧

A Strange Meal

Ezekiel 2:8–3:3 describes the prophet eating a scroll that contains God's words as a symbol of internalizing them. Ezekiel calls the scroll "as sweet as honey," which echoes the words of Psalm 119:103 (NIV): "How sweet are your words to my taste, sweeter than honey to my mouth!"

∽ 194 ∾

Swing Low, Sweet Chariot?

The old Negro spiritual by this title speaks (mistakenly) of the chariot that will take the believer home (to heaven). The image comes from 2 Kings 2:11, where Elijah was taken into heaven by a fiery chariot and fiery horses. However, the text actually says that Elijah was taken up in a whirlwind, not in the chariot itself.

∽ 195 ∾

A Festival of Remembrance

Passover, or the Feast of Unleavened Bread, was a spring festival associated with the barley harvest. It commemorated the Israelites' flight from Egypt, when God's angel of death passed over and spared the Israelites (but not the Egyptians), and when the Israelites fled so quickly that they had no time to let their bread rise.

∽ 196 ∾

Unicorns in the Bible?

The King James Version of the Bible mentions unicorns nine times. The actual animal is the oryx, a magnificent white horselike creature with two long, straight horns. It was hunted almost to extinction in the nineteenth century. Today it is slowly being restored in Israel by wildlife conservationists.

❧ **197** ❧

Rolling Away

The first place the Israelites encamped in the land of Canaan after they had crossed the Jordan River was Gilgal. They named the site "Gilgal" in a wordplay on the reproach of Egypt that was finally rolled away (Joshua 5:9). The Hebrew word for "to roll" is *galal*.

❧ **198** ❧

Donkeys

The donkey was one of the basic possessions of the ordinary Hebrew family. It was used for powering machinery to grind corn, for pulling simple plows, and for riding. It was an unclean animal, and thus not to be eaten, although during a siege of Samaria, a donkey's head was sold for food at a very high price (2 Kings 6:25).

❧ **199** ❧

Balaam's Donkey

Balaam holds the dubious distinction of being the only biblical character to have had a conversation with a donkey. Balaam was a prophet and magician who was hired by Balak, an enemy of Israel, to curse Israel. On his way there, his donkey balked at going on because it saw an angel and was fearful. The donkey even spoke to Balaam about this, according to Numbers 22:28–30.

∽ 200 ∾

Chariots of Fire

The Academy-Award-winning movie *Chariots of Fire* took its name from a biblical image, which was appropriate, since it was a story about a committed Christian runner. The image comes from 2 Kings 2:11, where a chariot of fire and horses of fire appeared and the prophet Elijah was taken up into heaven.

∽ 201 ∾

Kings and Donkeys

Several passages in the Old Testament speak of a king riding on a donkey. This is most striking in Zechariah 9:9, where it is prophesied that a king comes triumphant and victorious yet riding humbly on a donkey (and chariots and war horses are mentioned in the next verse). Jesus' entrance into Jerusalem fulfilled this prophecy (Matthew 21:5).

∽ 202 ∾

Unequally Yoked Animals

It was common in ancient times (as well as in modern times) to yoke an ox and a donkey together to pull a plow. However, Mosaic law prohibited this (Deuteronomy 22:10). While this may have been primarily for its moral lesson, it also was humane, since the two animals are not well matched for joint work.

➷ **203** ➶

Sycamore Figs

The prophet Amos was a "tender of sycamore fruit" by profession (Amos 7:14). The figs of the sycamore tree require cutting open with a knifepoint at a certain stage to help in the ripening process, and this is what Amos did.

➷ **204** ➶

Sheep

Hebrew has some 12 different words for sheep, such as ram, ewe, and flock. This undoubtedly reflects the important place sheep had in Israelite life and economy in Old Testament times. In the Bible, sheep are symbolically seen as innocent, sacrificial animals. Psalm 23 is one of the best-known passages to reference the animal: "The Lord is my shepherd; I shall not want" (verse 1).

➷ **205** ➶

Aaron's Rod

Moses' brother Aaron, the high priest, had a very interesting rod. On one occasion, it turned into a snake that devoured the Egyptian magicians' rods/snakes (Exodus 7:12). On another, it sprouted buds, blossoms, and almonds overnight; this was in a contest with the rebellious people concerning priestly authority (Numbers 17:8).

∽ 206 ∾
Bulls

Bulls were symbols of strength in most cultures in the ancient Near East. As such, they came to be objects of worship. Typically, the highest of the gods were represented as having bull-like features. Bulls adorned royal thrones, palaces, and temples. The Israelites fell prey to bull worship, building golden calves on at least two occasions.

∽ 207 ∾
Locusts

The eighth plague on Egypt was an incredible swarm of locusts, and the books of Joel and Revelation depict locusts as God's instruments of judgment. Even in modern times, swarms of locusts have darkened the skies and devastated areas up to 400 square miles.

∽ 208 ∾
Herbs and Spices

The Bible mentions about 15 to 20 herbs and spices, not all of which can be precisely identified. Some, such as cinnamon, stacte, and frankincense, were used to make sweet-smelling incense for religious purposes. Others, like mint, dill, cumin, and garlic, were used in preparing food. Still others, such as cassia and aloes, were used for cosmetics and medicines.

ᔟ **209** ᔟ

No Cupids Here

Cherubim, or cherubs, were winged creatures found in the tabernacle and temple. Two small cherubim flanked the mercy seat of the ark, two large ones flanked the ark itself in the temple, and cherubim were also woven into the fabric of the tabernacle and the great veil. Many artistic representations of cherubs survive from the ancient Near East, usually having some animal-like features, such as the body of a lion.

ᔟ **210** ᔟ

Fish

Fish were an abundant source of food in all Bible lands. The law of Moses (Deuteronomy 14:9–10) allowed eating whatever has "fins and scales" (most fish), but it prohibited eating whatever did not have these (thus excluding sharks, eels, and rays, and water mammals, reptiles, and invertebrates).

ᔟ **211** ᔟ

Sweet Cane

Isaiah 43:24 mentions sweet cane. A wild cane is found throughout Palestine, but most scholars think this refers to the sugarcane. Honey was the most important sweetener in Old Testament times, but this cane was probably chewed or used to sweeten drinks and food.

❧ 212 ☙

Illegitimate Temples

The temple Solomon built in Jerusalem was to be the one true sanctuary for Israel's worship. However, another Israelite temple was built at Arad in the Negev Desert during the same time. Jews at Elephantine, an island colony on the Upper Nile, also built a temple in the fifth century B.C., which incorporated worship of many gods, not just the biblical Yahweh.

❧ 213 ☙

Bees

The Bible mentions bees a number of times. Twice the swarming habits of honeybees are mentioned: Psalm 118:12 says that "[The nations] swarmed around me like bees," while Deuteronomy 1:44 mentions the Amorites chasing the Israelites like bees. The Hebrew word for "bee" is *deborah*.

❧ 214 ☙

The Ark of the Covenant

The ark was Israel's most holy object. It was an ornate box made of acacia wood, overlaid with gold, and topped with a golden mercy seat flanked by two winged cherubs. It contained the tablets of the Ten Commandments, a pot of manna, and Aaron's rod. It was kept in the Most Holy Place of the tabernacle and temple, but the Babylonians destroyed it in 586 B.C.

❧ 215 ❧

A Perfect Cube

The temple was carefully planned, including the details of its dimensions. It was an impressive structure, some 90 feet long, 45 feet wide, and 3 stories high. The innermost room, the Holy of Holies (or Most Holy Place), was where the ark of the covenant resided, symbolizing God's very presence. The ark's dimensions formed a perfect cube.

❧ 216 ❧

Ostriches

The ostrich was common in biblical lands, but today it is extinct there. It was used for food and for its feathers, and it is occasionally depicted in the art of Egypt and Assyria. Ostriches are described in considerable detail in Job 39:13–18, where their reputation for cruelty and stupidity is mentioned, as well as their blinding speed.

❧ 217 ❧

Lizards

Leviticus 11:29–30 mentions several animals that are unclean, most of them reptiles related to the lizard. They include "the large lizard... the gecko, the monitor lizard, the sand reptile, the sand lizard, and the chameleon." These all were among the "creeping things that creep on the earth." Lizards were (and are) common in Palestine.

❧ 218 ❧

An Excess of Gold

Much gold was used in Solomon's temple. The interior faces of the stonewalls were covered with fine wood and then overlaid with gold. The weight of gold coming in annually during Solomon's reign was 666 talents, or almost 50,000 pounds (1 Kings 10:14). In today's dollars, that would be worth almost $2.5 billion. Gold was so plentiful during Solomon's reign that silver was almost worthless.

❧ 219 ❧

Biblical Animals

The Bible mentions dozens of animals, wild and domestic, in many different contexts. Almost 180 Hebrew terms exist for animals, and more than 50 Greek terms. Unfortunately, not all the terms can be identified with certainty, and many animals have become extinct since biblical times.

❧ 220 ❧

Birds

The Bible mentions some 50 types of birds. More than 350 species of birds are identified today in Palestine. Birds are included among sacrificial animals and among clean (edible) and unclean animals. They can be found in numerous stories in the Bible, including the story of the doves and the raven of Noah's ark.

∽ **221** ∾

Doves and Pigeons

Doves and pigeons were the most important birds in the Old Testament. They were used often in sacrifices. When pigeons were used, they were always "young pigeons" (Leviticus 1:14). Noah sent out three doves from the ark to find land; the second brought back an olive leaf, a symbol of new life.

∽ **222** ∾

Owls

No fewer than eight species of owls have been tentatively identified from the lists of unclean birds in Leviticus and Deuteronomy, including the eagle owl, short- and long-eared owls, wood owl, fisher owl, screech owl, little owl, and scops owl. The eagle owl is the world's largest, measuring up to 28 inches long.

∽ **223** ∾

Name That Pillar

The temple had two tall freestanding bronze pillars at its entrance. Both had decorated bowls (possibly fire bowls) on top. The pillars stood more than 30 feet high, and both had names: *Jachin*, meaning "(God) will establish," and *Boaz*, meaning "in him is strength." When the Babylonians destroyed the temple, they took these away with them for valuable metal.

❧ **224** ❧

Biblical Festivals

Mosaic law established seven festivals. Three of these were great pilgrimage festivals that were related to the agricultural calendar: the feasts of Passover, Pentecost, and Tabernacles. The two high holy days (the Day of Atonement and New Year's Day) and two days of rest (the Sabbath and the New Moon festival) completed the festivals. The festivals of Purim and Hanukkah arose later.

❧ **225** ❧

Cranes

The crane is a beautiful, large wading bird, with long neck, legs, and bill, similar to a heron. It is mentioned twice in the Bible. Isaiah 38:14 mentions its noisy call, and Jeremiah 8:7 describes its regular migrating habits.

❧ **226** ❧

A Messy Affair

Worship at the temple was often messy business, since it involved killing and cutting up of so many sacrificial animals, including bulls, oxen, goats, sheep, and birds. When Solomon dedicated the temple, 22,000 oxen and 120,000 sheep were sacrificed according to 1 Kings 8:63. Sacrificial altars had special channels on the sides for carrying away all the blood.

∽ 227 ∾
Breaking the Sabbath

The Sabbath day was very important. Not only could people rest and be refreshed, but also they were reminded of God's Creation (Exodus 20:11). If people defiantly disobeyed God and worked on this day, the penalty was death (Exodus 31:15, 35:2). In fact, Numbers 15:32–36 tell of a man found gathering wood on the Sabbath who was stoned to death.

∽ 228 ∾
Partridges

The partridge is mentioned only twice in the Bible, once in reference to hunting it in the mountains (1 Samuel 26:20), and once in Jeremiah 17:11: "As a partridge that broods but does not hatch" like "he who gets riches, but not by right." The Hebrew word for partridge is *qore* ("one who calls"), referring to the distinctive sound it makes.

∽ 229 ∾
A Quiet Construction Site

The temple site was so holy that the raw building materials, including the huge stone blocks for the foundations and the walls, were prepared away from the site, and then brought to be installed in place. No tools—hammers, axes, or any iron tools—were heard on location, so that even the sounds of construction could not desecrate the site.

⨕ 230 ⨖

Synagogue Artwork

A stunning discovery was made in the 1930s of a synagogue at Dura-Europus in eastern Syria, which was completed in A.D. 255. Half of its walls were still standing, and they were decorated with many beautiful paintings of biblical scenes, including Abraham offering Isaac, Moses and the burning bush, and David playing his harp.

⨕ 231 ⨖

Ravens

The raven is the largest member of the crow family, and it is first encountered in the story of Noah's Flood (Genesis 8:7). It was one of the unclean animals (Leviticus 11:15). God's care for the raven was a symbol of his care for his people, and it also was a symbol of judgment and desolation.

⨕ 232 ⨖

Quail

Quail are mentioned in connection with only one event in the Bible. When the Israelites were in the wilderness, God sent quail into the camp in the evening and the people collected them for food. Quail are small game birds that migrate, but they can only do so with the help of the wind. The Bible states that they did come in on the wind (Numbers 11:31).

233

Snakes

Snakes are mentioned in the Bible mostly as symbols, usually as threats. Evil entered the world through Satan in the form of a snake (Genesis 3), and wicked people are often compared to snakes or their venom. The threat of great harm is often compared to a snakebite.

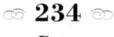

234

Deer

Several different words for deer are found in the Bible. The "hart" is probably the roe deer. The male of the species weighs up to 300 pounds and has six-pronged antlers. It is not well suited for desert living, which is reflected in Psalm 42:1 of the King James Version: "As the hart panteth after the water brooks..." The Bible usually mentions deer metaphorically, referring often to their graceful running and leaping abilities.

235

Purim

Purim is the joyful festival in the book of Esther, ordered by Mordechai to celebrate the Jews' great reversal of fortune. The Jews had been under an edict of death, and not only escaped this fate but also were able to kill their enemies. The events show an early example of the many tragic, state-sponsored persecutions that have been directed against the Jews.

∞ 236 ∞

Foxes

Foxes were well known in biblical lands. Their fondness for grapes is mentioned in Song of Solomon 2:15, and Judges 15:4–5 describes how Samson caught 300 foxes, tied them together with lighted torches between their tails, and sent them into the Philistines' fields. However, many scholars believe these actually were jackals, which are easier to catch.

∞ 237 ∞

Stalls and Stables

Several biblical passages mention stalls, which were the compartments animals were kept in within stables. King Solomon had 4,000 stalls for horses and chariots (2 Chronicles 9:25). Archaeological remains of impressive stables and stalls have been recovered from Megiddo and other cities, dating to later periods in Israel's monarchy.

∞ 238 ∞

Eagles

Eagles are mentioned more often than any bird of prey in the Bible. They are impressive for their great size, strength, speed, and soaring abilities. They are usually mentioned using stirring words, like in Isaiah 40:31: "But those who wait on the Lord shall renew their strength. They shall mount up with wings like eagles."

☜ **239** ☞

Horses

Horses were common in biblical lands. They are mentioned more than 140 times in scripture. In Old Testament times, royalty held horses, and they were a symbol of human power. In Israel, kings were not to accumulate horses, but to leave military matters to God. David kept a few horses after one battle, but his son Absalom was able to capture them during his revolt against his father.

☜ **240** ☞

The Lion's Den

A lion's den is mentioned in the story of Daniel, who was thrown into one when he refused to stop praying toward Jerusalem (Daniel 6:16–24). When he was vindicated, his false accusers and their families were themselves thrown in the den and devoured by lions. This practice was not known otherwise in the ancient Near East, but Job 38:39–40 does speak of lions crouching in their dens.

∽ 241 ∽

Bears

Bears are rare in today's biblical lands, but they are mentioned twice in Bible stories. The first is when David killed both bears and lions that threatened his sheep (1 Samuel 17:34–37). The second is a story about two bears that came out of the woods and mauled 42 boys who were tormenting the prophet Elijah (2 Kings 2:23–24).

∽ 242 ∽

Five Golden Mice

When the Philistines captured the ark of the covenant, God struck them with a plague manifested by an outbreak of tumors (1 Samuel 5). Mice or rats probably transmitted it. In response, the Philistines made five golden mice and five golden tumors and sent them into Israelite territory with the ark, hoping to stop the plague.

∽ 243 ∽

What Was a Nazirite?

Nazirites were people who took special voluntary vows to "separate themselves to the Lord" (Numbers 6:2). The vow included not drinking wine, not cutting one's hair, and not going near a dead body. Samson and Samuel were lifelong Old Testament Nazirites dedicated by their parents (although Samson violated all of the vows).

∽ 244 ∾

Cedars of Lebanon

King Solomon used wood from the stately cedars of Lebanon in making his temple. These trees can grow to a height of 120 feet, with a circumference of up to 40 feet. The wood is fragrant, free of knots, and is not attacked by insects. Although the once plentiful trees are now rare in Lebanon, they are the country's national emblem, appearing on its national flag.

∽ 245 ∾

Almond Trees

Joseph's father, Jacob, gave Joseph's brothers a present of rare delicacies that included almonds to take to their brother (Genesis 43:11). The tree's blooming in late January is a sign that spring is coming. Almonds served as models for the cups of the golden lampstand at the tabernacle.

∽ 246 ∾

The Sabbatical Year

The Law provided for the land to lie unplanted every seventh year (Exodus 23; Leviticus 25). This corresponded to the pattern of a weekly Sabbath for people, and it allowed the land needed time to rest. More importantly, whatever grew in the fields was to be left for the poor, and debts were canceled in the seventh year, allowing people a fresh start (Deuteronomy 15).

∞ **247** ∞

Pentecost

This feast was so named because it comes 50 days after the first Sabbath of Passover—*pent* means 50. It is also known as the Feast of Weeks, First Fruits, or Harvest. It was a spring festival celebrating the completing of the grain harvest.

∞ **248** ∞

No Crystal Balls

The prophets of the Bible were men and women sent by God to speak for him to the people. Contrary to a popular stereotype, their major role was not to be crystal-ball gazers, predicting the future for curiosity seekers. Rather, they were sent to address contemporary situations. They often had very harsh words to say to kings and people, and, as a result, were usually not very popular.

∞ **249** ∞

A Prophetic Showdown

A dramatic confrontation of a true and false prophet occurred between Jeremiah and Hananiah (Jeremiah 28). Hananiah claimed to speak for God, and he offered a soothing message to the people, while Jeremiah's message was much harsher. Jeremiah was vindicated when he correctly foretold Hananiah's imminent death.

∽ 250 ∾

Clean and Unclean

The Israelite ceremonial law went to great lengths to distinguish between the realms of clean and unclean, and to prescribe rituals of cleansing. Sources of uncleanliness included certain animals, bodily emissions, skin diseases (especially leprosy), and corpses. The basic purpose was to remind the Israelites of the gap between them and God. They needed to prepare themselves to meet with God, and they needed to do so properly and reverently.

∽ 251 ∾

Wild Boars and Pigs

Hebrew had only one word for domesticated pigs and wild boars. Both were on the lists of prohibited foods in Leviticus 11 and Deuteronomy 14. Psalm 80:13 refers clearly to the wild boar: "the boar out of the woods uproots [Israel]."

∽ 252 ∾

Dreams

Interpretation of dreams was an important means of discerning the will of God in biblical times. Every ancient king retained court wise men to interpret dreams. Joseph and Daniel are the best-known dream interpreters in the Bible. Daniel was even required to tell the Babylonian king what the king had dreamed, and then interpret it for him.

253

The Tree of Life

The tree of life is one of two special trees mentioned in Genesis 2. The other is the tree of the knowledge of good and evil. God placed the tree of life in the garden of Eden as a symbol of eternal life. After they sinned, God no longer allowed Adam and Eve access to it.

254

The Avenger of Blood

In many ancient societies, the relative of someone who was killed had the right to take vengeance for the death. Cain feared for his life because of this when he killed Abel. The law of Moses accommodated this practice, but carefully regulated it. The law distinguishes between accidental and deliberate homicide, provides cities of refuge, and requires approval of council elders before vengeance can be taken.

255

The World's First Clothes

Before Adam and Eve sinned, they did not wear clothes and they were not embarrassed. But after they sinned, they were ashamed and made clothes for themselves out of fig leaves, which were not very substantial. Later, God made them better clothes out of animal skins, which symbolized the animal sacrifices that would have to be offered for sin.

∽ 256 ∽

Waving Palm Branches

The four types of branches mentioned in Leviticus 23:40, which included palm branches, were to be held in one's hands during the reciting of the Hallel (Psalms 113—118), according to later Jewish custom. The palm branches were shaken three times in each direction of the four corners of earth, symbolizing the abundance that comes from God in heaven.

∽ 257 ∽

Foot Washing

Since people wore open sandals and traveled along dusty roads in Bible lands, their feet had to be washed frequently. This is mentioned several times in the Old Testament (see Genesis 18:4). Not washing one's feet was a sign of mourning (2 Samuel 19:24).

∽ 258 ∽

The Tabernacle of Meeting

This was another term for the tent. Its name indicates that it was a place where people could meet God. But there was also a separate tent called the "tabernacle of meeting" (Exodus 33:7). This was a temporary tent that Moses used to pitch outside of the camp, where he and the people could also meet God. It was not known later in Israel's history.

∽ 259 ∾

The Symbolism of Fish

Fish and fishing are mentioned symbolically many times in the Bible. Usually the imagery has to do with catching fish, whether with nets of otherwise. An example is Amos' jarring prophecy about Samaria's doom: "He will take you away with fishhooks, and your posterity with fishhooks" (Amos 4:2).

∽ 260 ∾

Sacred Meeting Places

Besides the temple and the tabernacle, there were certain other places where people could go to speak with priests. There was a temple of the Lord at Shiloh before Solomon's temple was built (1 Samuel 1). People also met at different times at Shechem, Bethel, Mizpah, Mounts Ebal and Gerizim, and many other places to worship God.

∽ 261 ∾

No Refuge

The altar of burnt offering had four horns (like the pointed horns of an animal such as a bull), one on each corner. These were considered the ultimate place of refuge and security. When the prophet Amos announced that even the horns of the altar at Bethel would be cut off, he was saying that there was no more escape for that wicked city (Amos 3:14).

∾ **262** ∾

Better Than Camping

The Hebrew patriarchs lived in large tents that were probably much like the tents used by modern Arab nomadic sheepherders. They are made of goat's-hair fabric, which keeps out rain and heat, and are large enough to contain two separate rooms—one for women and children, and one for men and guests.

∾ **263** ∾

A Lot of Lots

Many decisions in the Old Testament were made by drawing lots. The musicians in David's army "cast lots for their duty, the small as well as the great, the teacher with the student" (1 Chronicles 25:8). Nehemiah 10:34 speaks of casting lots to determine who would bring in a wood offering to the "house of our God." And Proverbs 18:18 gives a reason for the practice: "Casting lots causes contentions to cease."

∾ **264** ∾

Canaanite High God

Baal was the Canaanite god of storms and fertility, bringing rain and productivity to the land. His cult posed a greater threat to true worship in Israel than did any other cult, since the Israelites lived in closest contact with the Canaanites. King Ahab of Israel gave the first official sanction to worship Baal, an action that the prophet Elijah vigorously denounced.

∽ 265 ∽

Cave Hideouts

While there are many caves in Palestine, the Old Testament does not mention anyone living in them except in emergencies. Lot and his two daughters lived in a cave after Sodom and Gomorrah were destroyed. David and Elijah both hid in caves when their lives were in danger. And the prophet Obadiah hid 100 prophets of the Lord from the wicked queen Jezebel in two caves.

∽ 266 ∽

Ecstatic Frenzies

The Bible mentions some prophets practicing a form of prophecy in something like an ecstatic frenzy, accompanied by noisy musical instruments (1 Samuel 10:5–13). This phenomenon was well known throughout the ancient Near East. One Mesopotamian text speaks of the ravings of a *mahhu* (the Assyro-Babylonian title for ecstatic prophets) as follows: "I am smitten down like a mahhu. That which I do not know, I bring forth."

∞ 267 ∞

Elijah and the Prophets of Baal

Elijah had a dramatic confrontation with 400 prophets of Baal on Mount Carmel following a long drought. Elijah was able to call down fire from heaven, following which it began to rain. Baal's reputation was severely damaged because he had not brought fire or changed the weather, despite his prophets' desperate pleas.

∞ 268 ∞

Building Materials

Almost all Israelite houses during Old Testament times were made of mud bricks. The walls were coated with waterproof plaster on the inside. The floors were made of hard-packed clay, and wealthier homes had floors paved with smooth stones. Roofs were made from wooden beams covered in branches, which were filled in with mud plaster to make a flat surface.

∞ 269 ∞

Dagon: Baal's Father

Dagon was the principle Philistine god. He was the god of the storms and the grain harvest, whose temple Samson destroyed in his last acts of strength (Judges 16). Dagon was widely worshipped in all ancient Near East lands. In portions of the Baal mythology from Ugarit, Dagon was Baal's father.

❧ 270 ❧

Ancient Jewelry

Jewelry is mentioned often in the Bible, and much has been found in excavations of Bible lands. Early in history, it was made of bone chips, shells, and colored stones. Later, precious stones and metals were used more often. Many gold and silver necklaces, bracelets, earrings, and rings and beautiful precious stones have been found.

❧ 271 ❧

Rachel's Household Gods

When Rachel left her father's household after she married Jacob, she took with her the family's household gods and hid them under her saddle. Her father, Laban, was alarmed enough to come after her and retrieve them (Genesis 31). These were small idols kept in private households to consult about the future.

❧ 272 ❧

Head of the Household

Fathers were responsible for their whole households, including servants, in religious matters. Fathers were the ones who would bring the sacrifices to the priests. Joshua spoke for everyone in his household when he said that he and his house would serve the Lord (Joshua 24:15).

273

Planning for Disaster

Life in biblical times was tightly bound up with the cycle of the seasons and the availability of food. People lived with the worry that they were one bad year away from starvation. Joseph made a name for himself when he warned the pharaoh about an impending seven-year famine. He organized food storage and distribution programs to combat it (Genesis 41).

274

Times for Prayer

In biblical times, people prayed at any time of the day or night. There were formal prayers for morning and evening services in the temple. Daniel prayed three times a day in his bedroom. And Nehemiah prayed while he was working: Several times he uttered quick, impromptu prayers under his breath when a crisis arose.

275

A Generous Farmer

The law of Moses had many humane provisions for the poor, widows, orphans, and the like. One stated that farmers should not harvest every corner of their fields or vineyards, nor should they pick up what had fallen during the reaping process. These were to be left for the poor (Leviticus 19:9–10). We see Boaz putting this into practice in a heartwarming story in Ruth 2.

⤸ **276** ⤹

A Food Staple

Bread was an important food staple in Biblical times, and there are hundreds of references to bread in the Bible, over 20 in the book of Genesis alone. The word *bread* is often used to mean "food" in the Bible, as in Genesis 41:54, in the story of Joseph: "The famine was in all lands, but in the land of Egypt there was bread."

⤸ **277** ⤹

Draft Deferments

The Law provided for certain people to escape military service under certain circumstances (Deuteronomy 20). These included those who had built a house and not yet dedicated it, and those who had planted a vineyard and not yet enjoyed its fruits.

⤸ **278** ⤹

Storage Silos

Grain was stored in storage silos and barns in the ancient world. The Bible mentions full storehouses as being a blessing of God and empty ones as God's curse. An impressive underground stone-lined silo has been excavated from Megiddo, which was one of Solomon's store cities (1 Kings 9:19).

∞ **279** ∞

Follow the King

Priests were the primary religious authorities in Israel, but the kings also had religious duties. They were supposed to be examples for the people. They were to read and obey the Law and lead people in doing the same (Deuteronomy 17).

∞ **280** ∞

A Yearlong Honeymoon

Military exemptions applied to anyone who was engaged to be married (Deuteronomy 20:7). Furthermore, newlywed men were to be exempted from military service or any other business for a full year. This allowed for a good start to the marriage (24:5).

∞ **281** ∞

Not a Vegetarian

Meat was expensive food, served to guests only on very special occasions. Meat was common in royal palaces, however, because kings could afford it. The normal meat ration for one day in King Solomon's court was 10 oxen, 20 beef cows, 100 sheep, as well as deer, gazelles, roebucks, and game birds (1 Kings 4:23).

❧ 282 ❧

Mother of Life

Eve's name in Hebrew means "life" (*chavvah*). Adam called his wife "Eve, because she was the mother of all living" (Genesis 3:20). The word for "living" (Hebrew *chayyah*) is related to Eve's name.

❧ 283 ❧

Jewish Head Coverings

Jewish males traditionally have worn a skullcap for prayer and meals. This was regarded in the Talmud as a sign of reverence for God. Indeed, the Talmud indicates that rabbis did not walk even four steps with their head uncovered. This custom may have arisen from the priests' head covering mentioned in Exodus 28:37–39.

❧ 284 ❧

Abraham: Father of a Great Nation

Abraham's original name was Abram, which means "exalted father" or "the father is exalted." God gave him his new name, Abraham, which is explained as "father of a multitude." This was to emphasize God's promise to Abraham that he would have many descendants.

285

Manna

The Israelites were provided with "bread from heaven" in the wilderness. It appeared each morning as a fine, white, flaky substance on the ground that tasted like wafers and honey. Its name (Hebrew *man*) came from the puzzled Israelites, who asked "*man-hu*?" ("What is it?").

286

Oil Lamps

Oil lamps were the common means of lighting in biblical homes. They were made of clay or iron, and they burned olive oil for fuel. Thousands of oil lamps have been found from all periods. Early lamps were flat bowls, and then a spout began to evolve with a pinched edge at the rim. Later lamps had a hole for the wick.

287

Earthling?

Adam's name is related to the word for earth or ground (Hebrew *adamah*). Undoubtedly, this involves a play on words, since Adam was formed from "dust of the ground" (Genesis 2:7). Some modern works translate *Adam* as "earth creature" or "earthling" to emphasize this fact.

288

Biblical Merchants

Many different types of merchants produced products for sale, which were often sold at the city gate. In larger cities, tradespeople of the same trade lived in the same neighborhood. So there would be the potters' section of town, the food market, the cheese makers' valley, and so on. Nehemiah mentions the "Tower of the Ovens," which suggests bakeries clustered together (Nehemiah 3:11).

289

The Curse of Ham

One of Noah's sons, Ham, looked on his father inappropriately when his father was drunk and naked. For this, Noah pronounced a curse on his son. Some people have incorrectly seem Ham as the ancestor of the African peoples and made the wrong assumption that this was a curse on all black people.

290

World's First Warrior

Genesis 10:8–9 says that Nimrod was, "a mighty one on the earth. He was a mighty hunter before the Lord." He had a great kingdom that included several cities in Babylonia and Assyria. The Bible says that he built Nineveh as well.

∾ 291 ∾

A Season for War?

Ancient Near Eastern kings usually launched their military campaigns in the spring after the rainy season had ended. In Assyria, kings went out on a new campaign every year or two. Even the Bible mentions such a custom: "In the spring of the year, at the time when kings go out to battle..." (2 Samuel 11:1).

∾ 292 ∾

Biblical Barbers

The Old Testament records several actual incidents of cutting hair. Samson's lover Delilah betrayed him by having a man cut off his hair while Samson slept. Job shaved his head when he mourned. An Ammonite king humiliated David's servants by shaving half their beards. And Ezekiel was to shave his head and burn or scatter the hair in a symbolic act.

∾ 293 ∾

More Than One Ark

Hebrew has two words that are translated as "ark" in English. The most common refers to the ark of the covenant. The rarer word refers to Noah's ark and is also used for the basket of bulrushes that the baby Moses was placed into, Moses' ark.

⤶ **294** ⤷

Double Deception

Genesis 20 and 26 tell similar stories about Abraham and Isaac trying to pass off their wives as their sisters in Gerar, a Philistine city. This was for fear of the Philistine king, Abimelech, whom they thought would kill them in order to take their wives. The events were separated by many years, however, and the two Abimelechs may have been different people.

⤶ **295** ⤷

Respecting Dignity

In biblical times, if someone made a loan and a cloak or something else was put up as collateral, the lender was to respect the borrower's dignity by not entering his house to seize the collateral. He had to wait outside for the borrower to bring it out. If the borrower was poor, the lender also had to return the cloak each night, since that was what the borrower slept in (Deuteronomy 24:10–13).

⤶ **296** ⤷

Chariots: Ancient Tanks

Chariots were the ancient equivalents of modern-day tanks. They were very light, fast, and easily maneuverable. Chariot crews consisted of two to four men: a driver and one or more warriors, such as archers, spear throwers, and shield bearers. Chariots functioned best in flat terrain, so chariots are mentioned more often in flat Israel than in hilly Judah.

❧ 297 ❧

Feuding Brothers

Jacob and his twin brother, Esau, did not get along well for much of their lives, because Jacob took Esau's birthright. Their descendants were the Israelites and the Edomites, respectively, groups that continued to feud throughout their histories. The Bible states that this feud began even before the brothers were born: "The children struggled together within her [their mother Rebekah's womb]" (Genesis 25:22).

❧ 298 ❧

Childless Women

Several women in the Old Testament are described as childless at some point: Sarah, Rebekah, Rachel (all wives of the patriarchs), and Samson's mother, Hannah. In biblical times, being childless was a woman's greatest misfortune. However, each of these women was eventually given a child in the tradition expressed in Psalm 113:9: "He grants the barren woman a home, like a joyful mother of children."

299

Jacob Becomes Israel

Jacob wrestled one night with a stranger whom he recognized as God's representative, and he asked him for a blessing. The man then bestowed a new name upon him: Israel. This name means "he strives with God" or "God strives." It is based on a rare Hebrew form for striving (*yisar*) and one of the words for God (*El*).

300

Failed Magic

The Egyptian magicians in Moses' day were able to duplicate the first two plagues that God sent upon Egypt—turning the Nile to blood and producing frogs. They tried to duplicate the third plague—bringing forth gnats—but failed. They also were able to turn their rods into snakes, like Aaron did, but his "snake" devoured theirs.

301

An Iron Monopoly

During the Early Iron Age (1150–1000 B.C.), the Philistines were Israel's major enemy and they held a monopoly of iron in Palestine. In 1 Samuel 13:19–21, it states that there were no smiths in Israel. Whoever wanted to sharpen a plowshare or another tool had to go to Philistine territory, since the Philistines did not want the Israelites to make weapons.

∽ 302 ∾

Commemorative Pillars

The Hebrews used large standing stone slabs to commemorate important events or covenants. Jacob used a stone for a pillow at Bethel, and then set it up as a memorial of his encounter with God and poured oil on it. The Canaanites erected standing stones for worship, but the Israelites were prohibited from using these. An impressive set of 10 pillars still stands at a sacred Canaanite site at biblical Gezer.

∽ 303 ∾

Solomon's Bath

No, we aren't talking about how clean he was. The Hebrew *bath* was a unit of liquid measure, equal to almost six gallons (the royal bath was twice that). But the Hebrew word is not related to the English word. The large bronze "sea" in front of Solomon's temple had a capacity of 2,000 baths.

∽ 304 ∾

Achan and the Agony of Defeat

Achan was the man who caused the Israelites their only defeat when they entered the land of Canaan (Joshua 7). When they took Jericho, they were to set aside everything to God for destruction. However, Achan's greed got the best of him, and he hid some goods in his tent. As a result, Israel was defeated in their next battle, at the tiny outpost of Ai.

∽ **305** ∾

Ancient Well

The Hebrew patriarchs Abraham and Jacob dug numerous wells to provide water for their flocks. A remarkable well was excavated in the 1980s at Arad, in the Negev Desert of southern Israel. It is more than 10 feet wide and is neatly lined by stones to a depth of 68 feet at the water level. Water was carried from the well to a channel cut into rock that took water within the city walls.

∽ **306** ∾

Solomon's Chariot Cities

Solomon had Israel's greatest chariot forces. He had 1,400 chariots and 12,000 horses, which he imported from Egypt and Kue in Asia Minor (1 Kings 10:26–29). He established chariot cities where he could store his forces at Hazor, Megiddo, and Gezer.

∽ **307** ∾

Technology Transfer

By the early tenth century B.C., the military and technological tide had shifted in Palestine and the Philistines were no longer dominant, since Samuel, Saul, and David had subdued them. Archaeological evidence confirms this point—blacksmiths from northern Palestine were producing iron, while Philistine sites show no corresponding technological advances.

∽ **308** ∾

A Mother in Israel

Deborah is called "a mother in Israel" (Judges 5:7). In this context, it refers to her leadership over Israel. Israel had been quietly submitting to its enemies in those days, and it was not until Deborah arose as "a mother in Israel" that Israel began to have hope again. She provided the impetus and leadership for action and eventual victory.

∽ **309** ∾

Embalming

Embalming was not done in Israel; it was a distinctively Egyptian invention, and it was usually reserved for kings and persons of some repute. Two individuals are mentioned in the Bible as having been embalmed: Joseph, a Hebrew who had risen high in the Egyptian court, and his father, Jacob.

∽ **310** ∾

Teachable Moments

Israelite children would often ask their parents, "what does this mean?" when they saw memorial symbols, like the 12 stones Joshua set up to commemorate the crossing of the Jordan River (Joshua 4). Children would ask about the commandments of the Law (Deuteronomy 6) and the Passover feast (Exodus 12). In Jewish homes today, children still ask this question at Passover.

⊙ **311** ⊙

No Glory

Samuel's daughter-in-law gave birth to a son at a bad time in Israel's history, just after the ark of the covenant—which represented God's presence and glory—had been captured by the Philistines. Because of this, she named her son Ichabod, which means "there is no glory" or "where is the glory?"

⊙ **312** ⊙

Blessings

Jewish family life has always had a rich texture to it, and part of this involved the blessing of children by their parents. The Hebrew patriarchs Abraham, Isaac, and Jacob all blessed their sons, and the practice has continued to the present. A widely practiced custom today is the blessing of children at the Sabbath meal.

⊙ **313** ⊙

Hired Mourners?

The prophet Jeremiah speaks of professional women mourners who could be summoned in order to "take up a wailing for us." This skill was passed on to their daughters and even their neighbors (Jeremiah 9:17–20). But the Bible forbade anything too excessive: "You shall not cut yourselves nor shave the front of your head for the dead" (Deuteronomy 14:1). Israel's neighbors practiced these self-destructive customs.

∾ 314 ∾

Not Your Stereotypical Desert

For the most part, deserts in Bible lands do not have the great shifting sand dunes that are found in many deserts. Most of these deserts are dry, flat, and rocky. The hot desert winds blow fine dust or sand across the barren surface. Occasionally oases with springs and palm trees can be found.

∾ 315 ∾

Abraham's Rock?

A large rock measuring 58 feet long, 51 feet wide, and 4–6 feet high sits squarely in the middle of the Temple Mount. Different traditions say that this is the rock upon which Abraham offered his son Isaac as a sacrifice, where the great altar of Solomon's temple stood, and from where Mohammed ascended to heaven. Today, the Muslim Dome of the Rock stands over the spot.

∾ 316 ∾

The Philistines' Nemeses

Samson was responsible for the death of several thousand Philistines (Judges 14—16). This was helpful to the Israelites, since the Philistines were their major antagonists. Once, he even killed 1,000 men with the jawbone of a donkey. Shamgar was a lesser-known judge, but he too killed many Philistines: 600 of them with an ox goad (Judges 3:31).

∽ **317** ∾

Lot's Wife

As Lot and his family fled the destruction of Sodom and Gomorrah, Lot's wife turned to look back and was turned to a pillar of salt. The towering salt cliffs of Jebel Usdum (Mount Sodom) and the salt pillars at the southern end of the sea have been associated in tradition with this event. One distinctive 60-foot-high pillar is even called Lot's Wife.

∽ **318** ∾

Biblical Streaker

Isaiah walked through the streets of Jerusalem naked and barefoot for three years. He did this to make the point that Egypt and Ethiopia would be taken captive and humiliated, stripped naked and barefoot by the Assyrians (Isaiah 20:2–4).

∽ **319** ∾

Delilah

Delilah has become famous as a symbol of a treacherous seductress, since she was Samson's lover and the one who betrayed him to the Philistines. She did this by coaxing from him the secret to his great strength, which was his long hair (Judges 16). Contrary to popular thought, she did not cut his hair, but rather held his sleeping head on her lap while a man she called in cut it.

∽ **320** ∽

Gideon

Gideon was one of the heroes of the Bible: God gave him a great victory over the Midianites (Judges 7). He then properly refused an offer to make him king as a result. However, he was not perfect. He made an ephod—a garment worn by the high priest—and Israel committed idolatry by worshipping with it. Judges 8:27 states "it became a snare to Gideon and to his house."

∽ **321** ∽

The Bachelor Prophet

God told Jeremiah never to marry or have children, since conditions would soon become so awful in the land that children would die in great numbers and not be mourned or buried. This was because of the evil that had infested the land.

∽ **322** ∽

A Gracious Man

Jonathan, Saul's son, won an impressive victory over the Philistines at the Pass of Michmash (1 Samuel 14), and he rightfully aspired to succeed his father as king. However, when it became clear that God had rejected his father's claim to the throne and that David would become king, he held no grudge and enthusiastically supported David.

∽ **323** ∾

Searching for Noah

Many modern-day expeditions have searched for Noah's ark on the snow– and glacier-covered slopes of Mount Ararat, a 17,000-foot peak in Armenia, in eastern Turkey. However, the Bible says that the ark came to rest on "the mountains of Ararat" (Genesis 8:4), which may mean anywhere in mountainous Armenia.

∽ **324** ∾

Above the Hills

The term Mount Zion originally referred to the low hill of Jerusalem on which King David built his early city. Later, it was transferred to a higher hill to the west. It came to symbolize the capital of God's kingdom, and Isaiah and Micah spoke of Mount Zion as ultimately being established "on the top of the mountains... exalted above the hills" (Isaiah 2:2; Micah 4:1).

∽ **325** ∾

Saul and the Medium at Endor

Early in his reign, King Saul had tried to rid the land of mediums and wizards. However, late in life, when God no longer answered his inquiries, he used the services of a medium to inquire about his upcoming battle with the Philistines. The medium called up Samuel from the dead, who was disturbed at being called, but who prophesied Saul's death (1 Samuel 28).

❧ **326** ❧

A Hidden Water Tunnel

The Jebusites, who lived in Jerusalem before King David, were responsible for an ingenious tunnel system that brought fresh water into their city. They tunneled straight down through a hill above a spring and tapped into an underground stream. They lowered buckets and filled them from this stream and did not have to go outside the protection of the city walls.

❧ **327** ❧

Breath of God

The prophet Amos speaks of God roaring like a lion from Jerusalem because he is angry at the nation of Israel and the blast of his roar causing the top of Mount Carmel to wither. Mount Carmel is a lush, wooded mountain more than 70 miles north of Jerusalem. God's breath not only reaches Carmel, but it scorches the shepherd's pastures along the way (Amos 1:2).

❧ **328** ❧

Rebellious Sons

Several important characters in the Bible had sons who turned out badly. The two sons of Aaron, the high priest, offered unsanctioned sacrifices (Leviticus 10). The two sons of Eli the priest abused their priestly position and were called worthless men (1 Samuel 2). Samuel's two sons took bribes and perverted justice (1 Samuel 8).

∽ **329** ∾

Goliath Wasn't the Only Giant

Og, king of Bashan (an area northeast of the Jordan River), opposed the Israelites when they wanted to pass through his land (Deuteronomy 3). He was a giant of a man. His bed was made of iron, and it was on display in Rabbah, capital of the Ammonites, for many years. It was more than 13 feet long and 6 feet wide!

∽ **330** ∾

City of Shalom

When the Israelites took over Jerusalem, its many gods and pagan culture offended them, and so they gave its name a new meaning, "City of Peace" (*Shalom*). This was possible because its name sounds just like the Hebrew words for "city of peace." This title has remained a symbol of people's hopes for the city ever since.

∽ **331** ∾

A Man of Shame

2 Samuel 2 calls Saul's son *Ishbosheth*, which means "man of shame." But 1 Chronicles 8:33 gives his name as *Eshbaal*, which means "man of Baal." He was probably born as Eshbaal. However, the author of 2 Samuel substituted the name meaning "man of shame," rather than honor a pagan god by using the other name.

∽ **332** ∾

Kings Like No Others

Hezekiah and Josiah were among Judah's greatest kings. 2 Kings 18:5 states that Hezekiah was incomparable: Hezekiah "trusted in the Lord God of Israel, so that after him was none like him among all the kings of Judah, nor were before him." Josiah was incomparable also: "Neither before nor after Josiah was there a king like him" (2 Kings 23:25, NIV).

∽ **333** ∾

Test of Champions

When David met Goliath in a one-on-one confrontation, they were engaging in a relatively uncommon "contest of champions." Each army would pick its best warrior to do battle. The winning side was determined by the results of this contest, thereby avoiding much bloodshed and death. However, when David killed Goliath, the Israelites pursued and killed many Philistines, despite the ground rules.

❧ **334** ❧
Goliath's Spear

Goliath's spear is described as being "like a weaver's beam." This meant that it had a leash of cord wrapped around the spear shaft, with a loop into which he inserted his fingers. This was similar to a weaver's beam, which was a block of wood attached to a cord for separating threads. This styling would give the spear a spin, and thus a longer and truer trajectory.

❧ **335** ❧
The Duties of a King

Deuteronomy 17:14–20 lists the qualifications and duties of a king: God must choose him, he must be an Israelite, he must not multiply horses for himself (i.e., rely on his army, with its horses and chariots), he must not multiply wives (who might turn his heart away from God), he must not accumulate too much wealth, and he must know and keep the Law.

❧ **336** ❧
Nabal, the Calebite

Nabal was an unfortunate man. His first name means "fool," and his surname means "dog" (dogs were despised creatures in the ancient Near East). Nabal lived up to his name in his foolish dealings with David, and eventually he drank himself to death (1 Samuel 25).

☙ **337** ☙

A True Friendship

David and one of Saul's sons, Jonathan, made a pact that they would remain loyal to each other and each other's posterity (1 Samuel 20). After Jonathan died, David inquired about his relatives. Mephibosheth, who was crippled, was the only one left, so David took him in like a son (2 Samuel 9).

☙ **338** ☙

Water Through a Rock

One of the great engineering feats recorded in the Bible was the 1,750-foot-long tunnel—through bedrock 150 feet under the City of David in Jerusalem—that was dug during King Hezekiah's reign. It provided water from a hidden spring, which would be helpful in time of siege. It was laboriously hacked out of the rock with pickaxes by two crews digging toward each other.

☙ **339** ☙

Impressing the Queen

After she had heard of Solomon's fame, the queen of Sheba came from her kingdom in southern Arabia or northeast Africa to test Solomon with hard questions (1 Kings 10). He impressed her with his great wisdom, knowledge, and wealth, so she honored him with huge quantities of expensive gifts.

➰ 340 ➰

A Jewish Hero with a Pagan Name

Mordechai and Esther are the two heroes of the book of Esther. Mordechai is honored by the Persian king and placed in the highest position in the land. Ironically, he is named for a Babylonian god, Marduk. It occurs in an extra-biblical list of Persian dignitaries as "Mardukka."

➰ 341 ➰

Man of Peace

Solomon's name (Hebrew *Shelomo*) means "peace" (*shalom*), and it reflected God's promises about his kingdom. David was told that he should not build the temple in Jerusalem, because he was a man of war. Instead, God said, "A son shall be born to you, who shall be a man of rest … I will give peace and quietness to Israel in his days" (1 Chronicles 22:9).

➰ 342 ➰

Jehoiachin in Babylon

The Bible records that the last king of Judah, Jehoiachin, was treated humanely while he was living in exile in Babylon (2 Kings 25:27–30). The Babylonian king freed him from prison, gave him a prestigious post among captured kings, and invited him to dine daily at the king's table. In this way, 2 Kings ends with hope for the future of God's people.

∽ **343** ∽

A "Solomonic Decision"

This phrase refers to a decision in a difficult judicial case that brilliantly reveals the truth or finds some middle ground. It comes from a case Solomon faced, where two women argued over the same baby. His solution was to cut the baby in half. The imposter was happy with this arrangement, but the true mother revealed herself by refusing and offering to let the other woman have the baby (1 Kings 3).

∽ **344** ∽

Bittersweet Naomi

Naomi, Ruth's mother-in-law, lost her husband and her two sons. Her name means "pleasant," but she told people to call her *Mara*, which means "bitter" (Ruth 1:20). Fortunately, in the end, things were pleasant for Ruth and Naomi.

∽ **345** ∽

Who Is Buried in Absalom's Tomb?

The old joke about who is buried in Grant's tomb takes on new meaning in Jerusalem. A five-story-high rocky monolith east of the Old City of Jerusalem is called Absalom's Tomb. However, Absalom, a son of David, is not buried here. The tomb probably got its name because of a biblical reference to a monument that Absalom built for himself.

⤳ 346 ⤶

The City of David

The city that David captured from the Jebusites and lived in was small, about 15 acres in size. It was a walled city built on a low, elongated hill, next to which was a hidden spring. It was a significant city despite its size, and David was able to use many of the existing buildings and bureaucracy in setting up his kingdom.

⤳ 347 ⤶

Feathery Hair

The book of Daniel tells of King Nebuchadnezzar's being humbled by God. He was driven away from Babylon into the fields, where he lived with the beasts of the field and ate grass like cattle. "His body was wet with the dew of heaven till his hair had grown like eagles' feathers and his nails like birds' claws" (Daniel 4:33).

⤳ 348 ⤶

How David Captured Jerusalem

Jerusalem's water supply was its weak point, and David exploited that in capturing the city. He challenged his men to "use the water shaft" which they did, either by cutting off the water supply or by going up the tunnel itself into the city (2 Samuel 5:7–9, NIV).

∽ 349 ∾

Alexander the Goat

In one of Daniel's visions, he saw an accurate picture of Alexander the Great and his empire. He reported seeing a goat with "a notable horn between his eyes… The male goat grew very great; but when he became strong, the large horn was broken, and in place of it four notable ones came up toward the four winds of heaven" (Daniel 8:5–8).

∽ 350 ∾

Ancient Undergrad?

The King James Version states that the prophetess Huldah lived "in Jerusalem in the college" (2 Kings 22:14). This results from a misunderstanding of the Hebrew term *mishneh* (literally, "second"), which most modern versions translate as "Second Quarter" or "Second District." This area of Jerusalem was on the hill west of the Temple Mount.

∽ 351 ∾

A Reluctant Prophet

When the prophet Amos protested that he was not a prophet nor a prophet's son (Amos 7:14), he meant that he had not been raised or trained as a prophet, and he did not make his living prophesying. Rather, he had his own profession, and he was prophesying only because God had sent him on a special mission.

❧ 352 ❧
A Real Wordsmith

On 38 occasions, Ezekiel used a very pejorative word for idols in the Old Testament: *gillul*. This word combines the vowels of the word for "sacrilege, abomination" (*shiqqush*) with the consonants of the word for "dung pellets" (*galal*). The resulting word means "idol" (but it is not the usual word for idol), and it expresses a special disgust for these objects.

❧ 353 ❧
Unusual Weather

Snow was (and is) rare in Bible lands, limited mainly to the high mountain ranges. Only one time is actual snowfall mentioned, but it was remembered in the same way that today we would remember outstanding storms. One of King David's warriors killed a lion "on a snowy day" (2 Samuel 23:20).

❧ 354 ❧
Jericho: The World's Oldest City

A spring waters Jericho, which was first occupied in 9000 B.C. It was an oasis in the Jordan Valley, and was called the City of Palms in the Bible. The Israelites captured it under Joshua, in the famous incident when its walls collapsed.

❧ 355 ❧

An Immortal Duo

Only two characters in the Bible never died: Enoch and Elijah. "Enoch walked with God; and he was not, for God took him" (Genesis 5:24). Elijah the prophet was taken to heaven in a fiery chariot without dying (2 Kings 2).

❧ 356 ❧

A Curse Fulfilled

Joshua's curse on Jericho stated that anyone rebuilding Jericho would pay a stiff price: "At the cost of his firstborn son he shall lay its foundation, and at the cost of his youngest he shall set up its gates" (Joshua 6:26, NRSV). Many years later, a man named Hiel, from Bethel, did some rebuilding, and it cost him his oldest and youngest sons, in fulfillment of this prophecy (1 Kings 16:34).

❧ 357 ❧

Where Was Tarshish?

The book of Jonah states that Jonah took a ship going to Tarshish rather than go to Nineveh, as God had commanded him. Tarshish was either part of the island of Sardinia (off the coast of Italy) or a region in far-off Spain. It is obvious that Jonah's intent was to go as far away from Nineveh as he could.

⊙ 358 ⊙

Solar and Lunar Eclipses

The Bible mentions eclipses several times, as prophetic signs of God's judgment. Amos 8:9 states, "I will make the sun go down at noon, and I will darken the earth in broad daylight." Joel 2:31 says, "The sun shall be turned into darkness, and the moon into blood." Lunar eclipses do indeed look red at times, due to refraction of the sun's light.

⊙ 359 ⊙

Son of My Sorrow

Rachel was Jacob's beloved wife, and she bore him Joseph and Benjamin, his two favorite sons. However, she died giving birth to Benjamin. As he was born, she named him *Benoni* which means "son of my sorrow," but he was renamed Benjamin ("son of the right hand") by his father (Genesis 35).

⊙ 360 ⊙

The Ancient of Days

This is a title given to God in Daniel 7, describing the last judgment. God is described as enthroned on a fiery throne, with snow-white clothing and hair white like pure wool. It is an elegant description for an old man, and it emphasizes God's eternal nature as it contrasts with the earthly kingdoms described in the chapter.

❧ 361 ☙

Widowed Without Mourning

God took Ezekiel's wife, the "delight of his eyes," from him, but Ezekiel was instructed not to mourn, weep, or make any public display for her. This was to foreshadow God's destroying the temple, the "delight of Judah's eyes," which Judah was not to mourn, since Judah had so greatly profaned it and its worship.

❧ 362 ☙

Singing and Dancing

Singing and dancing were essential components of the worship of God. The Israelites celebrated many victories with excited singing and dancing, and often women led the way. David danced a joyful and frenzied dance when the ark entered Jerusalem. Great choirs led singing in the temple courts.

❧ 363 ☙

The Cave of Machpelah

This was the cave that Abraham bought to bury his wife Sarah in, near Hebron (Genesis 23). Abraham, Isaac, and Jacob also were buried there. Abraham's purchase was significant, since it represented the first clear title to the land that God had promised him. A mosque marks the spot of this cave today.

☙ 364 ☜

The Khamsin

A hot south and east wind blows across Egypt and Palestine during the months of May and October. It fills the air with dust and often lasts three days or more. The Bible mentions this wind many times as a symbol of God's wrath. Isaiah describes how God removed his people into exile: "With his fierce blast he drives her out, as on a day the east wind blows" (Isaiah 27:8, NIV).

☙ 365 ☜

Dumb Hicks?

Every faith has had backsliders and followers in name only. The agnostic or irreligious Jews of biblical times were called *Am ha'aretz*. It means "people of the land"—but perhaps "dumb hicks" better conveys educated Jews' distain for their ignorant country cousins. The term is in use today, though its meaning has evolved to mean a Jew who is lax in Jewish observance, while still implying ignorance.